THE CAT & THE BANKER

HOW TO GET STARTED WITH INVESTING: AN ILLUSTRATED STORY

NADIR MEHADJI

Marshall Cavendish
Business

Illustrations copyright © 2018 by Nadir Mehadji
Cover design by Marcel Heijnen

Published by Marshall Cavendish Business
An imprint of Marshall Cavendish International

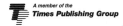
A member of the
Times Publishing Group

Other Marshall Cavendish Offices:
Marshall Cavendish Corporation. 99 White Plains Road, Tarrytown NY 10591-9001, USA • Marshall Cavendish International (Thailand) Co Ltd. 253 Asoke, 12th Flr, Sukhumvit 21 Road, Klongtoey Nua, Wattana, Bangkok 10110, Thailand • Marshall Cavendish (Malaysia) Sdn Bhd, Times Subang, Lot 46, Subang Hi-Tech Industrial Park, Batu Tiga, 40000 Shah Alam, Selangor Darul Ehsan, Malaysia

Marshall Cavendish is a registered trademark of Times Publishing Limited.

National Library Board, Singapore Cataloguing in Publication Data

Name(s): Mehadji, Nadir.
Title: The cat & the banker : how to get started with investing : an illustrated story / Nadir Mehadji.
Other title(s): Cat and the banker : how to get started with investing | How to get started with investing : an illustrated story
Description: Singapore : Marshall Cavendish Business, 2017. | The ampersand in the title is outlined to represent a cat.
Identifier(s): OCN 1008623326 | ISBN 978-981-4794-44-2 (paperback)
Subject(s): LCSH: Investments--Popular works. | Portfolio management--Popular works. | Finance, Personal--Popular works.
Classification: DDC 332.678--dc23

Printed in Singapore by Markono Print Media Pte Ltd.

TO ECHO

CONTENTS

MICELAND

- CURRENCY: THE MICKEY
- POPULATION: NOT SURE

PENGUIN BAY

OUR STORY
HAPPENS HERE

CATLAND

DOGLAND

- CURRENCY: DOGLAR
- POPULATION: LOTS

- CURRENCY: CATDOLLAR
- POPULATION: MODERATE

INTRO:

HOUSTON, WE HAVE A PROBLEM

Socrates Cat rolled over onto his belly as the *ping* of a message notification took him out of his slumber. He opened one eye and saw the message flashing: "LAST WARNING. Spending limit exceeded. AGAIN. Get your act together. NOW." He pondered the thought for a second and dozed off again.

A year earlier, Socrates' life had changed dramatically when he received inheritance money from his uncle Apollo. Both of them had always been close. A successful technologist, Apollo had invented the Catbot, an artificially intelligent device that spoke Meowsic. The Catbot allowed felines to interact with their phones without having to type; a revolution in Catland and a major upgrade from Bluefang technology. Catland, despite being a small country, had a thriving economy, although its ballooning banking sector was a cause for concern. With his invention, Apollo acquired instant fame. He also made good money, incidentally.

Apollo's will stated that he would hand down his possessions to his nephew Socrates, his closest family. That's how Socrates inherited the small fortune of C$150,000, the catdollar (C$) being the local currency in Catland. Socrates' life changed overnight. He had been working as a freelance designer until then and freelancing had been a rough ride. Now, fat fish, mouse mousse and milk nectar were his diet on lean days.

But all wasn't rosy. When Socrates finally got up, he reluctantly looked at his finances. The graph showing his savings looked like a sinking ship. The thing is Socrates did enjoy the good life; he was a cat after all. He thought of former pawgilist champion Cat Tyson, who had squandered a larger fortune and now lived like a stray cat in his old days. Not the way to go. Socrates knew that he had to do things differently if he wanted a comfortable future. He needed to make his money grow.

As Socrates took his wallet, a photo slipped out. It was a picture of him and his uncle that had been placed with the will. As the photo lay face down on the floor, Socrates noticed a small note on the back. He'd missed it before. "Don't blow the money, invest it," Apollo had written. "And call PiggyBank," he had underscored, "the only bank with a half-decent reputation. Make an appointment with a financial catviser."

"Is that it…?!" Socrates thought.

Socrates called the bank and explained that he was considering investing a sum of money. The clerk replied that they'd be delighted to discuss his circumstances.

This was how cat Socrates embarked on his investment odyssey. He was scheduled to meet with PiggyBank the next day.

A GIFT TO MICE

INFLATION

Socrates received a warm welcome at PiggyBank. He was ushered into a meeting room bathed in natural light. A tall bottle of branded milk stood on the table.

Socrates had stopped by the grocery store to buy a couple of cans of fish on his way to the bank. He placed his groceries on the seat next to him.

"It is a pleasure to meet you, Mr Cat," the banker said with poise as he entered the room. "How should I address you?"

"You can call me Socrates."

"I'm Catsby."

Catsby was an unusual sight in Catland. He was a lion. "I understand that you would like to make investments," he said.

"I'd like to invest C$100,000 or so. But I have limited knowledge. I'm not sure how to approach investing. I don't know where to start. I was hoping you could help me."

"I'm glad you came," Catsby said. "You know Socrates, there was a time when I wasn't much of an investor myself. But I became a good investor after I understood the six different types of investments and when to invest in them. We will talk about that as I teach you the ropes.

But first things first. Everyone has their own objectives when it comes to what they want to achieve with money.

My role is to try and understand what your objectives are and to help you make investment decisions that you are comfortable with.

Generally cats who come here seek one of three things, or a combination of them.

The first is to preserve the value of their wealth.

The second is to generate regular income.

The third thing is to grow their wealth.

You will need to think about which of these you want to achieve. So tell me, how does having money make you feel?"

"It gives me peace of mind," Socrates replied.

"Money makes us feel safe, doesn't it? It is tempting to keep it in a stash close to us. You know, hidden in a cardboard box, or in a ball of wool, or in a bank account. But if we don't invest our money, it tends to lose value over time."

"How could I lose money by putting it in a safe place?" Socrates asked.

Catsby pointed at the grocery bag on the chair. He could see its contents. "May I ask how much you paid for the cans of fish?"

"C$2 a can," Socrates replied.

"How much do you think a can cost five years ago?"

"Around C$1?"

"Sounds like a fair guess. So the obvious thing would be to say that the price went up, right?"

Socrates nodded.

"Another way to see it is that the value of a can hasn't changed. A can of fish is still worth a can of fish.

Your money however is now worth twice as little. The same dollar today only buys you half a can. In other words, the value of the catdollar has shrunk."

Socrates hadn't quite realised the implication until now.

"There is a word to describe the phenomenon of prices rising. It is called inflation. And just as inflation measures how fast prices are going up, inflation also measures the pace at which the value of your money depreciates."

Socrates looked concerned. "How do you measure inflation?" he asked.

"Inflation in Catland ran at 2% last year. It means that the price of things are on average 2% more expensive than they were a year ago. What it really means for you though, as you have savings, is that inflation makes you poorer as time goes by."

Catsby took a notepad and drew a chart. "The bite of inflation can be nasty. If you do nothing about your money, at a 2% annual inflation rate, in 10 years, your C$100,000 will have the same value as $82,000 only. If inflation runs faster still, at 5%, your $100,000 will be worth about $60,000 in 10 years. And at 10%, your $100,000 will have less value than $40,000 then.

Inflation may be silent. But its impact is real. Holding onto money in times of inflation is not a good idea."

"Losing money to inflation sounds treacherous," Socrates said. "It's like giving money to mice to nibble. I want my savings to grow, not dwindle!"

"Then we need to find ways to make your money grow by at least the future rate of inflation, just to preserve the value of the savings that you currently have. We need to find better stores of value than just holding onto catdollars."

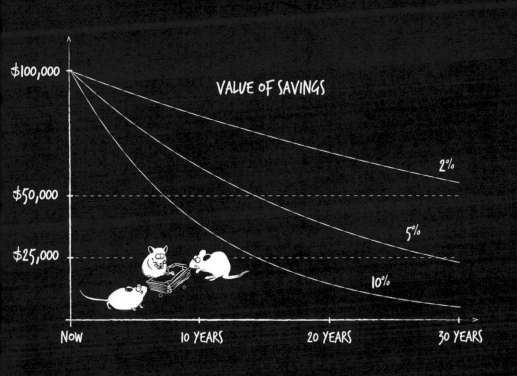

Socrates was pensive. He was pondering the issues of money for the first time. Now that he had savings, he had to worry about seeing them evaporate...

"Let's meet again tomorrow if you like," Catsby said.

HOW TO START INVESTING
– JOURNEY MAP –

1 UNDERSTAND YOUR OWN OBJECTIVES & CIRCUMSTANCES

2 UNDERSTAND HOW THE BUILDING BLOCKS OF INVESTING WORK & WHAT THEY DO

3 UNDERSTAND HOW THE BUILDING BLOCKS REACT TO EXPECTATIONS FOR THE ECONOMY & HOW THEY FIT WITH YOUR OWN OBJECTIVES

4 START SMALL. EXPERIMENT. FIND OUT WHAT YOU ARE COMFORTABLE WITH, SO YOU CAN DO IT YOUR WAY

(NO WORRIES... CATSBY WILL HELP YOU WITH THESE STEPS)

THE MENU

PORTFOLIO, RETURNS & ASSET CLASSES

Socrates returned to PiggyBank the next day. Catsby was waiting for him.

"I thought about my objectives," Socrates said, "I want to grow the value of my money, but I also want to derive some income from it. How should I invest my C$100,000?"

Catsby smiled as he was anticipating the question. "We have a whole toolbox of investment products for you to choose from. Let me show you."

Catsby took a folder and placed a document in front of Socrates. The document read: "The Building Blocks of an Investment Portfolio".

"What is a portfolio?" Socrates asked.

"A portfolio is a word we use to describe a collection of investments.

At the moment, your portfolio consists of your C$100,000, which you hold in cash. In other words, you are already invested. And you are all invested in cash. But over time you may decide to convert some of it into other types of investments.

You could think of your portfolio as a wallet where you keep track of all the things that you have invested in."

"How do I go about creating a portfolio?" Socrates carried on.

"We will need to choose suitable investments. But there are two sides to every investment. Choosing investments is a trade-off between the returns that you expect to reap and the risks that you take."

"What exactly do you mean by return?" Socrates asked candidly.

"When we invest, our goal is to make a profit on the money invested, right?

However, we need an objective yardstick to measure the performance of our investments.

A return is the gain or the loss that we make over a particular period of time, as a percentage of the money we invested initially."

"I see," Socrates said.

Catsby continued: "The return of an investment has two components: income, and capital gain or loss.

Say that you used your C$100,000 to purchase a flat. You manage to rent it out and obtain C$4,000 in rent the first year.

At the end of the year, you manage to sell the flat for C$110,000.

The overall profit on your investment would be:

– C$4,000 in rent, which counts as "income" as it is money that you collected while you owned the investment, and

– C$10,000 of profit on the sale of the flat, which counts as capital gain. The capital gain or loss is the profit or loss that an investor makes when the investment is eventually sold, compared to the price he originally paid for it.

That is a total profit of $14,000, from both income and capital gain, over the $100,000 that you initially invested.

THE 2 COMPONENTS OF RETURNS

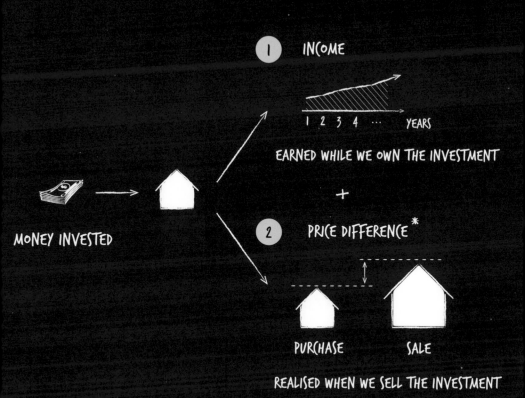

1 INCOME

1 2 3 4 ... YEARS

EARNED WHILE WE OWN THE INVESTMENT

+

2 PRICE DIFFERENCE*

MONEY INVESTED

PURCHASE   SALE

REALISED WHEN WE SELL THE INVESTMENT

* THE TECHNICAL TERM IS "CAPITAL GAIN OR LOSS"

Your return would be the ratio of the two numbers: 14% over one year."

"I get it," Socrates said.

"One thing however," Catsby added. "If you remember, we spoke about the dangers of inflation yesterday."

Socrates nodded.

"The return on investment which really matters is not the apparent return. What matters is the net return that you earn after you strip off the effect of inflation."

Socrates looked perplexed.

"How much did you earn last year on your savings at the bank?" Catsby asked.

"About 2.5% interest," Socrates replied.

"But inflation ran at 2% last year. So you did not actually become 2.5% wealthier.

Given that life is now 2% more expensive on average, the wealth on

KEEPING IT REAL...

APPARENT RETURN[*] — INFLATION = REAL RETURN

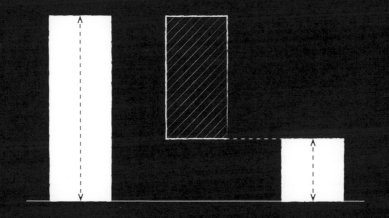

[*] THE TECHNICAL TERM FOR THE APPARENT RETURN IS THE "NOMINAL" RETURN

your bank account only grew by 0.5%, the difference between the interest rate that you earned and past inflation.

That net return of 0.5% is called the real return, as opposed to the apparent return of 2.5%.

Many investors forget about the difference between apparent returns and real returns. Apparent returns sometimes give the impression of getting richer. But we can only know whether we are better off once we consider real returns."

"Keep it real..." Socrates thought.

"How about the document that you were going to show me?" he asked.

"The building blocks of an investment portfolio? Take a look at page two."

Socrates flipped the page. It looked like a menu, under an underscored title that read "Asset Classes".

"What is an asset class?" Socrates asked.

"An asset is something that you own and has value. It is just another name for an investment.

THE BUILDING BLOCKS OF AN INVESTMENT PORTFOLIO

ASSET CLASSES

1. STOCKS
2. BONDS
3. REAL ESTATE
4. CURRENCIES
5. COMMODITIES
6. ALTERNATIVE STORES OF VALUE

Organising investments in separate asset classes is a way of classifying different types of investments according to features and behaviours that they share in common.

For example, investing in land or investing in a house are close, so both go into the same category called real estate.

"Like different boxes?" Socrates asked.

"Like different boxes," Catsby confirmed.

Socrates quickly browsed through the menu. A lot of the names of the asset classes were alien to him. "Those asset classes sound like exotic birds."

Catsby smiled. "We will go through the list together now. But there's no need to remember every detail. Just get familiar with the names for now. It will come in handy later."

Catsby started reading: "Among asset classes, we find...

1. Stocks:
Stocks are a share of ownership in a company. Stocks give an investor the right to receive a share of the profits that a company makes. The share of profits that a company pays to an investor is called a dividend. Stocks are also known as shares or equity.

2. Bonds:

Bonds are loans. They regularly pay an investor fixed amounts of money called coupons according to a pre-defined schedule.

There are two broad categories of bonds: government bonds, when an investor lends to a country, and corporate bonds, when an investor lends to a company.

3. Real estate:

Real estate includes land and buildings. Real estate pays investors rent. Real estate is also known as property.

4. Currencies:

A currency is the money that a particular country issues. Different countries have different currencies. The national currency of Catland is the catdollar, while Dogland, the neighbouring country, uses the doglar.

5. Commodities:

Commodities are raw materials, such as agricultural products, metals or energy, which are consumed or used in manufacturing.

6. Alternative stores of value:

Alternative stores of value are valuable objects, such as fine art, antiques, jewels, collectibles, or precious metals like gold."

Catsby folded the document and put it in his pocket.

"Can I invest in any of those?" Socrates Cat asked.

"If you wish," Catsby replied. "But we should first look into how they work. This way you will understand which ones suit you better, and what to expect from each.

Besides, you mentioned that your investment objectives are to generate both growth and income. But this is only part of the answer. Investing is not one-size-fits-all. It needs to be tailored to your own circumstances. So we will do a little test at our next meeting."

OK, COMPUTER

PERSONAL CIRCUMSTANCES, SNOWBALLING & THE MAGIC NUMBER 69

Socrates went back to the bank intrigued to hear more. He had caught a glimpse of the investment menu. But Catsby wasn't about to let him order yet.

"Are you ready for the test?" Catsby asked.

"Sure. But what is it about?"

"This little test will help us determine which investments are more suitable for you considering your personal circumstances. Different investments imply various types and levels of risk." Catsby got up and went to a computer in a corner of the room. "Please join me at the computer. We will need to answer a few questions."

It looked like an old IBM computer. Socrates looked puzzled about how to use it.

Catsby said: "I'm sorry, you will need to use the keyboard. The mouse keeps running away."

The screen displayed the first question: "In order of preference, do you care more about: maximising gains, minimising losses, or both equally?"

Catsby clarified: "This is to get a sense of how you would react if you lost money. There is no right or wrong answer. But if you know that you hate losing, it is better not to get into investments whose returns can vary wildly, and instead look for investments that have tamer potential gains and losses. Regardless, it is not recommended to invest money that you cannot afford to lose."

Socrates thought about his answer for a moment: "I'm not averse to taking risks. At the same time, now that I have some savings, I would like to preserve them as much as possible. It would hurt if I lost them all. So both maximising gains and minimising losses equally is my preferred answer."

The next question was: "What is your age?"

Catsby said: "Age is an important consideration when assessing how much risk we should take. When we are young, we can afford to take greater risks. Time is our friend. But we should become more conservative as we get older. When we lose money later on in life, we may no longer have time or circumstances on our side to make up for it. So it is prudent to gradually convert our riskier investments into safer ones as we age. I suppose this is not a concern for you yet, though, Socrates. You are still a fine young cat."

Socrates grinned.

The computer beeped. "What is your investment horizon?" Catsby reworded the question: "How long do you intend to wait before reaping the fruits of your investments?"

"Ten years or so? But I would also like to generate some income in the meantime."

"That's nice. Ten years gives us time," Catsby said. "The longer our time horizon, the more risk we can take. If the price of an investment drops temporarily, we may have time to wait for it to recover, while investors with a shorter time horizon might be pressed to sell at a loss. We can also afford not to let short-term swings in the price of our investments sway our mood, as long as we agree with the logic and the outlook that led us to make those investments in the first place."

"Do you intend to stay in Catland?" the computer asked next.

"Nosy programme," Socrates thought. "My plans aren't quite set. But for now, I do. Why is the computer asking?"

"We need to define your base currency," Catsby said.

"My base currency?"

"It is the currency in which the returns of your investments will be calculated. Typically your base currency is the currency in which you will spend the money that you earned from your investments. Since you plan on staying in Catland, your base currency is the catdollar.

This won't prevent you from investing abroad. For instance, the economy of our neighbouring country, Dogland, has done very well lately and you might wish to consider investing there.

But the reason why we need to clearly define your base currency is this: if you decided to invest in Dogland, we would need to be mindful of the possible fluctuations in the exchange rate between catdollars and doglars. These currency fluctuations will affect your returns."

Socrates pressed the "Feed me" key to validate his answers. The computer made a buzzy-hum cranky noise as it printed a ticket.

"OK, computer... That's a 7!" Catsby said.

"What does it mean?"

"On a scale from 1 to 10, where 1 represents the most conservative attitude to risk and 10 the most fearless, the computer thinks that you could be 7. It suggests that you can take moderate risks. Knowing this will help us decide which kinds of investments are more suitable for you."

They went back to the meeting table.

"Would you like some catnip?" Catsby asked.

"No, no, thank you."

"You are lucky to have this money to invest early on, Socrates."

"How is that?"

"When money can earn a return, time is your friend, because returns work for you in an interesting way."

Catsby grabbed a notepad on the table and drew two lines. One curved and rising, the other one straight.

He pointed at the curved and rising line: "If you do the right thing, the returns that you earn on money over time will not grow in a straight line. Instead they will accelerate and snowball. We normally use the word 'compound', but snowball is also a good word."

"How does it work?"

"Say you manage to earn 10% returns on your investments every year, C$100,000 invested would become C$110,000 after a year, right?

Then you would need to make a decision with important implications: whether to reinvest the returns or not."

"Why?"

"If you decide to spend returns every year instead of reinvesting them, you would earn C$10,000 each year, or C$300,000 in total over 30 years, and at the end of 30 years, the C$100,000 originally invested would remain at C$100,000."

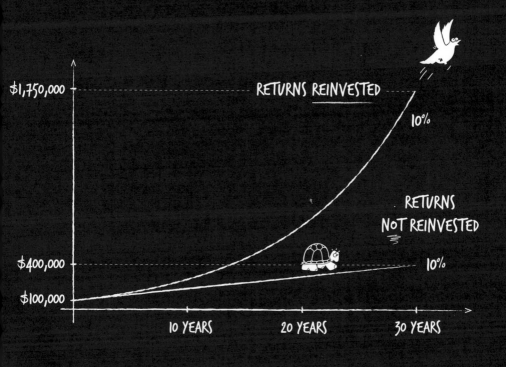

"OK."

"If you decide to reinvest the returns that you earned the first year instead of spending it, then the second year you would make 10%, not only on the original C$100,000, but also on the C$10,000 that you reinvested. New returns would build up over old returns.

If you did that consistently over thirty years, C$100,000 invested at a steady annual return of 10% would grow almost 17 times... It would become $1,744,940!

Over a long enough period of time, the snowballing effect of returns can grow even a small amount into a large sum."

"It sounds powerful..."

"This is also why starting to invest early and earning slow but steady returns might sometimes be a better strategy than earning money fast one year and losing money another year. Managing to avoid losing money can go a long way when combined with the compounding effect of returns."

"How long would it take me to double my C$100,000 if I reinvested returns every year?" Socrates asked.

"It's simple. Let me give you a trick. The magic number is 69.

Say you made 2% annual returns and you reinvested your returns, to calculate how fast you could make C$100,000 become C$200,000, you would simply divide the magic number 69 by 2, the return."

"That would be about 35 years?" Socrates said.

"Indeed. If you earned a bit more, say 5%, you would simply divide 69 by 5. It would take about 14 years.

How about if you earned 10%?" Catsby asked.

"69 divided by 10?" Socrates said.

"That's right. About 7 years. Easy, no?

"I like it."

Socrates and Catsby had not noticed that night was falling. The room was darker now.

"It's getting late. We will start looking into asset classes in more detail next time we meet."

The meeting left Socrates wondering. After he inherited Apollo's money, Socrates thought that investing would be straightforward. He'd ask a financial adviser what to do and it would be sorted. He now realised that there were many factors to weigh in. It was like he had opened a can of worms. A good one though.

INTERMISSION:

DREAM ON

Socrates couldn't meet Catsby the next day. He had an appointment with a client of his own to pitch an exciting design project.

WoolsWoof, the client, was a Dogland company. They specialised in balls made of sheep wool. Cats loved them and Catland was a large target market.

The brief for the project was to design a new logo for the brand; something that conveyed a sense of playfulness, endless entertainment and innovative engineering.

Socrates met the CEO himself, Herman Shepherd, and four of his sidekicks.

Socrates presented the concept behind his designs with bravado and panache. He explained his creative process, showed the client prototypes and the many ways WoolsWoof could replicate them through their various product lines.

Shepherd looked thoroughly impressed and so did the rest of the team. However the atmosphere felt slightly off.

Shepherd broke the uncomfortable silence: "Listen, Socrates, we are truly impressed. This is actually really good. Your logos are witty and inventive. The budget is in the right ballpark."

"But...?" Socrates already dreaded a lame excuse.

"This is a huge project. And your ideas are big, but we need to know how you're going to implement them. How many team members did you say you have?"

"It's just me, but I've successfully managed projects like this before!"

"We don't want you to get stretched," Shepherd said.

"I'm flexible."

"Listen... be reasonable. It's a tough world out there. Why don't you expand, Socrates? And you'll be on our panel to compete for the next project."

The CEO and his team left the room.

Socrates felt rage boiling up. He was ready to pounce and tear down the room. But then he remembered his mum saying, "It's cool Socrates, it's cool" and managed a couple of yoga breaths.

So he thought: "Keep it real... next time."

THE RIGHT TOOL FOR THE RIGHT JOB

EQUITY & DEBT

"A dog's life," Socrates grumbled as he headed to his meeting with Catsby.

"Do you mind if we go for a walk?" Catsby asked when his client arrived. Unlike Socrates, he seemed to be in a cheerful mood.

Socrates didn't mind. In fact, it was a welcome thing to do after the previous day's incident. So they went out. Catsby stopped to buy a copy of the *Black Cat Bone*, the local newspaper. The front page was all about Fat Fish Company, the famous canned fish manufacturer. They were celebrating their 25th anniversary.

"Have you ever run a company?" Catsby asked Socrates.

"I run my own design studio. But it's mostly a one-cat-show."

"Design? So I suppose you haven't found the need to raise money to expand your business yet?"

"Well, that didn't seem necessary until... yesterday," Socrates confessed. "I haven't thought about how I would do it either."

"Then you may find this useful in the future. Let me tell you what other business owners do when they need external financing to grow their business."

"Is this relevant to my investments?"

"Very much so," Catsby said, as he opened the newspaper. "Do you know about Fat Fish Company?"

"Who doesn't?"

"I like them," Catsby said. "Once we're back in the office, I will tell you how Fat Fish became a large company. And you will understand how the two most common asset classes, stocks and bonds, come from how businesses grow and finance themselves."

They headed back to the bank.

"Two founders started Fat Fish Company," Catsby said.

They opened their first fish-processing factory by the harbour near this office.

Business took off quickly, and soon the two founders realised that they needed more money to finance their expansion.

When reinvesting the early profits of Fat Fish Company was no longer enough to keep growing, the founders looked for external investors to put money in their business.

Fat Fish could resort to raising two types of financing.

One is called equity. This is money from investors who want to own a stake in a company.

The other one is debt: money from investors who agree to lend for a given period of time.

Over time, Fat Fish used both to finance the growth of its operations."

Catsby took a sheet of paper and drew a box. He split it vertically in the middle.

THE FAT FISH COMPANY
BUYS & MAKES ALL THIS...

THANKS TO THAT

FAT FISH COMPANY

 BUILDINGS

 FACTORIES

 MACHINES

 CANS OF FISH

 RAW FISH

 CASH

EQUITY

MONEY FAT FISH
OWES TO ITS OWNERS

 +

DEBT

MONEY FAT FISH
OWES TO ITS LENDERS

"You can represent a company like this," he said.

"On the left is what a company owns: its assets.

On the right is what the company owes: its liabilities.

Equity and debt are on the right side, because eventually, the company owes that money to the investors who gave the company its financial resources."

"How did Fat Fish raise equity and debt?" Socrates asked.

"In order to raise equity, the founders of Fat Fish literally sold shares of their company. Investors who wanted to have a stake in the business could own a portion of the company in exchange for money: they could buy "shares".

Shares are titles of ownership which prove that investors own a stake in the company. That's why owners of a business are also called shareholders."

"That makes sense. How about debt?"

"Fat Fish also borrowed money to finance the development of its operations. Initially they needed relatively small amounts. So Fat Fish could borrow money from banks which granted it loans.

As Fat Fish started borrowing larger amounts of money to sustain their ever growing operations, they could no longer rely on banks alone for loans.

So Fat Fish Company also started borrowing money from individual investors, like you and me. And they did that by issuing bonds."

"What are bonds?"

"Bonds are loans which are sliced into small pieces.

This way, any investor – no matter how small and not just banks – can lend money."

"Smart. So bondholders are lenders?"

"That's right. When an investor buys a bond, he owns a portion of a bigger loan.

But unlike shareholders, bondholders do not own the business. They only lend money temporarily against the promise of future repayment and the payment of some interest on the way."

"I see the difference."

"Mind you, the jargon of investing can be confusing sometimes.

A number of terms are used interchangeably. Just remember that 'equity' means the same as 'shares' and 'stocks', and that both 'loans' and 'bonds' are forms of debt."

"OK."

"Now, there is a reason why I took this little detour to explain how Fat Fish Company grew. Understanding how stocks and bonds relate to businesses should later help us understand why the value of stocks and bonds change over time.

Investing is not disconnected from what is happening in the economy, far from it.

A lot of financial products are by construction related to the actual economy. Despite this, they sometimes seem to have a life of their own.

It looks like a contradiction. But in due time I will explain why it makes sense. It has to do with expectations."

"Sure. You said earlier that stocks and bonds are the most common asset classes. Are they the best?"

"They are the most commonly talked-about asset classes. But no asset class per se is better than another asset class.

You could think of asset classes as tools. They are tools for different jobs. And depending on the job that you want to do, it makes sense to choose different tools."

"Tools for what, for instance?" Socrates asked.

"Do you remember how returns have two components: income and capital gains?

Different asset classes provide potential income and capital gains in different proportions and with different levels of certainty.

For instance, some asset classes, like bonds or property, can provide regular income. Others, like stocks, provide erratic income. Others yet, like commodities, provide no income at all and are all about prospective capital gains."

Catsby drew a table where he listed the split between income and resale value for different asset classes.

"On top of that, different asset classes perform best in different sorts of economic circumstances. So you could also see asset classes as tools to express a view on a particular set of economic conditions that you anticipate.

But we will talk about that later."

INCOME VS POTENTIAL CAPITAL APPRECIATION

	INCOME	VS	POTENTIAL CAPITAL GAIN OR LOSS AT TIME OF SALE
STOCKS	✓ DIVIDENDS		✓
BONDS	✓ COUPONS		✓
REAL ESTATE	✓ RENT		✓
CURRENCIES	✗		✓
COMMODITIES	✗		✓
COLLECTIBLES	✗		✓

Socrates realised that Catsby saw the world of money differently. If Catsby had been a character in a role-playing game, he would have seen investments as different sorts of weapons, each with certain strengths and weaknesses.

Some weapons were designed for attack, but offered little protection. Others were good at defence, but would never inflict much damage. What you chose would be a matter of preference, strategy and circumstance.

LOCKED, STOCKS & A BLOWN BARREL

STOCKS

Socrates Cat picked up a copy of the *Black Cat Bone* at the newsstand on the way to his next meeting with Catsby.

The front page covered the up-and-coming start-up, Snapcat. They had developed an app for felines to post felfies on the social network, Vimeow. Their business plan was to generate revenue through advertising.

Socrates expected that Catsby would start diving deeper into individual asset classes at the meeting.

"Are we going to talk about stocks and bonds in more details today?"

Socrates asked right off the bat.

Catsby smiled. "Stocks are on today's agenda. Let's see if we have time for bonds. Are we in a rush?"

"Time is money," Socrates said as he slammed the door of the meeting room behind him. The handle fell off. Socrates looked away, pretending it wasn't him.

"Now we're trapped. That's good. We won't get distracted," Catsby said as he suppressed a laugh. "But let me call a locksmith or we'll still be in here tomorrow.

Stocks are the first stop on our list of asset classes.

Do you remember how the two founders of Fat Fish got outside investors to buy stakes in the company when they needed more money to grow?

The first time that Fat Fish sold shares to raise money, the company issued one million shares. Each share was sold at a price of C$5. I remember because I bought some at the time.

As I bought shares in Fat Fish, I became one of the company's many owners. And I gave C$5 to the company for every share I bought.

The shares sold quickly, and the founders of Fat Fish were able to raise C$5 million of fresh funds by giving up part of their ownership of the company to external investors.

Some shareholders decided to sell their shares, as they no longer wanted to be involved in the future of the company. Their shares were put on the market and other investors were happy to replace them.

Things were a little different this time round though. When the original owner of a share sold his share to the next investor, the money did not go to Fat Fish any more. Instead, the money went to the seller of a share.

In fact, the company received fresh money only the first time the shares were issued. All subsequent exchanges of shares would only be transfers of ownership from one seller to the next buyer. And those transactions are of no relevance to Fat Fish Company. It is only accountable to the last holder of a share, no matter who that is."

"Why did you decide to buy shares?" Socrates asked.

"I bought shares because I wanted to buy into a business.

Shareholders are business owners. And owners have a right to receive a share of the future profits of the company.

So a shareholder who invests in a stock of Fat Fish Company buys the prospect that the business will make growing profits."

"You mean that stocks are about the future?"

"Yes, stocks are simply bets on the future profits of a business.

What investors express when they buy a share is a particular view on the future profits that a company may make."

"What price should you be ready to pay for a stock?" Socrates asked.

"The value of a stock is the sum of all of the future profits that a company will ever make, divided by the number of shares in the company."

Socrates tried to imagine a stack of all the future profits Fat Fish Company would ever return. That seemed like a lot. He said: "So the price of a Fat Fish share reflects the profits that investors anticipate the company will make this year, next year, and all subsequent years?"

"That is exactly right," Catsby said, "with a slight but important nuance, however. You mentioned that time is money earlier today, right?"

"I did."

"This is a core principle at the heart of investing."

"How so?"

"Let me ask you this: would you prefer to receive one dollar today or in a year's time?"

"Today. No question," Socrates said. "Why would I want to wait?"

"In the context of investing, 'time is money' means exactly this. Money is worth less the longer you have to wait for it."

"Is this related to the fact that inflation will erode the value of C\$1 received in a year?" Socrates asked.

"To some extent, because it's hard to know in advance the exact value that C\$1 received a year from now will have after inflation.

But that's not all. There is also a certain degree of uncertainty around receiving money a long time from now. Conditions might change and the profit that you anticipate might not materialise after all. Instead, the .C$1 that you receive today can be reinvested straight away.

So, back to your question about the value of a stock. When we assess how much a stock is worth, we need to take into consideration the fact that time is money and that far away profits are less valuable than close profits. As a consequence, profits expected far away in time need to be depreciated to reflect their diminished value compared to earlier profits."

"So when investors buy stocks, they pay for the future, but not the very distant future?"

"That is an insightful way to put it. The value of a stock reflects the future of a business, and the near future more so than the distant future.

The fact that stock prices are all about the future also implies that stock prices can move up or down even if present conditions do not seem to change materially. That's because stock prices are not about what is happening right now.

Instead, they change in line with the anticipated profits that a company will make. As anticipations change, prices change."

"So changes in stock prices are about changes in people's perception?"

"Yes. And this is true of investing in general, not just for stocks.

You sometimes see that some investors get excited and rush to buy stocks when the economy is booming and then turn gloomy and sell when the economy is down.

This behaviour assumes that stock prices should keep going up when the present situation looks bright and keep going down when the present situation looks bleak.

But you may have noticed that stock markets sometimes go up even though the economy remains in the doldrums. Other times stock prices plummet while the economy is still expanding.

That's because in the first case, investors have already started anticipating a recovery, and what rising stock prices reveal is increasingly upbeat expectations about the future. In the second case, investors preempt the economy losing momentum even as it is still running fine."

"So investors need to be one step ahead?" Socrates asked.

"Yes. The two questions for a savvy investor are: what anticipations are already reflected in the stock price, and how may anticipations change?"

"Betting on the future sounds like gambling," Socrates pointed out.

"You might view it that way," Catsby said, "but the analogy between stock investing and gambling is a bit inaccurate."

"How so?"

"Could you recall a gambling situation?" Catsby asked.

"Sure. I used to go to the annual rat race with my uncle Apollo. One day he bet on a crazed rat, Under Mouse, that nobody thought would win. But the rat crossed the finish line first. Apollo beat everybody else."

"That's a nice memory. But see, when Apollo won, he did not make his money from any of the rats in the race. Instead, his prize money came from other players who lost their bet, right?"

"Correct."

"Investing in assets that pay income works slightly differently.

You see, for instance, when you buy a stock and bet on a company, you do not always need other investors to validate your bet. You can make money from the company itself.

We briefly mentioned when we went through the list of asset classes that stocks pay a type of income called the dividend."

"What is a dividend?" Socrates asked.

"Suppose that you bought a Fat Fish stock. Every year that Fat Fish Company makes a profit, the top management decides to distribute a portion of the annual profits to shareholders, the owners of the company.

That portion of the profits is called the dividend. It is paid evenly across shares. So each stock receives an equal share of the dividend.

The portion of the profits that the company does not distribute is reinvested in the company, to help the business grow the following year."

"Understood."

"As one of the first investors in Fat Fish, I bought stocks for C$5. It turned out to be a bargain. Fat Fish has since paid me that in dividends many times over.

When an investor buys a stock, the bet that he makes is effectively whether the company's future profits will match the anticipations that the stock price reflected when he bought the stock.

Since, over a long enough period of time, the company will pay the profits that it makes to the owners of the company via dividends, the question is: is the current stock price below the estimated value of the company's future profits?

If an investor thinks so, he should buy the stock and collect dividends year after year, or wait for the stock price to correct to what he perceives is its fair price.

If on the contrary, the stock price exceeds the company's estimated future profits, the investor is better off selling the stock to another investor if he can, and by doing this, he collects his prize money from other 'players'. "

"I see how the sanction of a stock investor's bet can come from the company itself, rather than exclusively from other players in the game," Socrates said.

Catsby and Socrates heard three knocks. They looked towards the door.

A voice barked: "Stay away, keep clear!"

They looked at each other.

Then smoke came out of the keyhole.

"That's a locksmith from Dogland," Catsby said.

An explosion blew the door open. Debris flew through the room like a shattered barrel.

A BOTTLE OF MILK

LIQUIDITY

"All clear!" the locksmith cheered. But he was gone before Socrates or Catsby could see through the cloud of dust. They were so surprised that neither of them had run for cover.

Catsby looked unfazed. But the computer in the corner was trashed. "Animal," he said.

"Does it matter what proportion of the profits a company pays as a dividend?" Socrates coughed, as the dust settled.

"For the price of a stock, not majorly," Catsby replied, cool as ever.

"Different companies have different policies regarding what

percentage of their profits they distribute as dividends to their shareholders.

Fat Fish Company is now a mature business for instance. It no longer grows fast and it returns steady profits year after year. So Fat Fish pays most of its profits as dividends. The company no longer needs to reinvest them.

But there was a time when Fat Fish was a young and fast-growing company, like Snapcat for example. Do you know Snapcat?"

"Yes, they were in the news today."

"Snapcat does not pay dividends. As a young company, they need to dedicate every cent to expanding.

But this is not necessarily an issue for shareholders. Shareholders pocket the dividend if a dividend is paid. But if no dividend is paid, it means that the profits stay in the company they own. Either way, the money is theirs, directly or indirectly.

As long as the company remains profitable, reinvests its profits in order to grow and generates greater profits in the future, both the company and its owners benefit eventually.

What shareholders buy in a stock is the company's capacity to generate greater profits over time. If not right now, a bit later."

"How do you know how much profit a company will make?"

"Stocks do certain things very well. They are a great way of benefiting from future business and economic growth. But stocks do other things poorly. They offer limited visibility on the timing of future income.

Shareholders have no guarantee of return. The exact profits that a company will make are hard to predict, so the dividends that a company will pay shareholders are uncertain. It takes research to form opinions about the prospects of a company."

"You mentioned that you can sell a stock?" Socrates said.

"A shareholder can sell his stocks. But he can't be certain about the future price that he will sell it for. The resale price of a stock depends on the price at which the next buyer will purchase it."

"So shareholders have both upside potential on their investment as well as downside risk?" Socrates asked.

"That's right. Stocks are unstable, and a shareholder is exposed to both the good and bad fortunes of a company."

"Are we just betting on a company when we buy stocks?"

"Companies do not operate in a vacuum," Catsby replied. "They are also sensitive to what the economy is doing.

A company might be able to ride an expanding sector of the economy, or benefit from an overall expanding economy. So when the whole economy grows, a well-run company may see its profits lift like a boat on a rising tide.

So buying stocks is also an indirect way of gaining exposure to the ups and downs of the entire economy."

"Which companies should I buy shares of?" Socrates asked.

"Companies with prospects of growing profits become more valuable over time. Conversely, stocks of companies whose profits keep deteriorating fall as time goes.

Identifying the first kind of companies requires homework. But when an investor buys a stock, he buys into a business. He needs to understand how the business makes money and how it plans to grow.

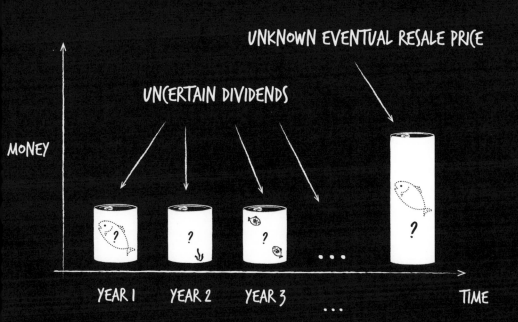

Besides, which stocks to buy may also depend on your own investment objectives. There is no best stock for every investor.

Stocks whose earnings are expected to grow at a high rate are better for capital appreciation. They are known as growth stocks.

Stocks of companies that enjoy steady business and generate stable profits are better for income, as those companies are able to pay investors regular dividends. They are called income stocks.

Other stocks are neither. Stay away from those."

"How would you observe the difference between growth and income stocks?"

"You could look at the dividend yield the stock provides. It is the ratio between the dividend that the company pays and the current price of the stock. It measures how much income the stock pays as a percentage of the stock price."

"So Snapcat would qualify as a growth stock, while Fat Fish would be an income stock?" Socrates asked.

"Very much so."

"Could I buy shares in Snapcat?" Socrates asked.

"Well, you could, but you need to know that while all stocks pretty much work the same, there is a difference between the stocks of public and private companies. Snapcat is a private company."

"What is the difference between public and private companies?"

"Public companies are listed on a stock exchange, a marketplace where stocks are traded.

The main stock exchange in Catland is the Catland Stock Exchange, also known as the "CatSE". Anybody can buy shares of companies listed on an exchange.

Fat Fish is listed on the CatSE. But Snapcat, as a young private company, isn't. Generally, private companies are either too small to justify being listed on an exchange, or they prefer to stay in private hands.

If you still want to invest in Snapcat however, you could negotiate with the management team directly. And if you manage to become an early investor, you need to know that selling the stocks of a private company is complicated.

Remember how the handle just fell off the door and we got trapped in here? When you buy a private company, you may be locked in your investment until the company becomes listed on an exchange."

"Questions around selling should be taken seriously, it seems," Socrates said.

"How easy it is to get out of an investment is a question that investors need to ask for all asset classes. A savvy investor takes into account the liquidity of an investment."

"Liquidity...?" Socrates' gaze shifted to the milk bottle on the table.

Catsby noticed and smiled. "Liquidity here has got nothing to do with... you know. Instead, it describes how easily an investment can be bought or sold quickly without affecting its price.

An investment is liquid when you can sell it at short notice without having to concede a large discount to the next buyer.

Typically, houses are illiquid investments. They take time to sell, unless sellers offer a heavy rebate. And in the case of stocks, private stocks are significantly less liquid than the stocks of public companies."

"Lots of things to consider when investing in stocks," Socrates said.

"Stocks are a risky type of investment. They have both high upside potential and high downside risk. But it also depends on which companies you look at.

Snapcat is a fast growing company, with a highly unknown future trajectory. But other companies offer investors better visibility over their more stable market and their future earnings. What makes a company risky is the lack of predictability of its future profits."

"Since I can't invest in Snapcat, could I put all of my money in Fat Fish shares?" Socrates asked.

"I would not recommend that."

"Why...? The company is established and you like it."

Catsby laughed. "It has nothing to do with whether I like Fat Fish or not. My concern is about timing and concentration. Remind me to tell you about two practices to manage risk tomorrow."

"What are they?"

"The first one is diversifying, when it comes to the composition of your investment portfolio. The second one is scaling into investments, when it comes to the timing of your purchases."

"I am not sure what you mean," Socrates said.

"I know. But don't worry. It will all be clearer tomorrow. Also, bring your swimsuit. I think you deserve a break. The weather tomorrow should be beautiful. I'll take you on a boat trip to Penguin Bay."

INTERMISSION:

A WET CAT

Socrates was drawn to the headline of the *Black Cat Bone*: "Fat Fish stock down 20%!"

In shock, Socrates scanned the article: "Fat Fish Company reported earnings after the market close yesterday. Financial results disappointed analysts. The management blamed this year's lacklustre results on the changing tastes of young customers. Millennial cats prefer broccoli. The stock opened 20% lower on the CatSE today. The price had been stable for a month."

Socrates sighed in relief. "Luckily Catsby stopped me from rushing to buy yesterday."

"I was surprised when you talked me out of buying Fat Fish shares. Now I'm grateful that I didn't jump into it," Socrates told Catsby when they met.

"The fall in Fat Fish stocks might be a temporary dip," Catsby said. "We don't know.

What I meant yesterday is that diversifying is the proverbial 'do not put all your mackerels in the same bucket'.

Putting all your money in a single investment is a very concentrated decision. Your money is then tied to whatever might happen to this particular asset."

"So diversifying is better?"

"Not always better, but certainly more prudent. Diversifying across various investments will make your investment portfolio more resilient to unforeseen circumstances. What happens to a particular investment would have less impact on the overall health of your entire portfolio.

Some investors are very good at making winning decisions. But not even the best investors know the future. Predicting which investments will do well over time is no easy task."

"How do you diversify?"

"Diversifying is about buying different kinds of investments which are unlikely to all go up or down at the same time.

You could diversify within one asset class. For instance, you could buy shares of companies from different sectors of the economy: some Fat Fish shares in the food sector and some Cat & Pillar shares in the construction sector.

You could also diversify across various asset classes. You could for example buy stocks, bonds and property. Investments in different asset classes are by definition less correlated than investments within the same asset class.

You could also diversify geographically. You could make some investments in Catland and others in Dogland.

And you could mix and match these different approaches for greater effect."

"Yesterday, you also mentioned something like... fish scales?"

Catsby coughed. "Actually, what I mentioned was 'scaling in'..."

Socrates blushed.

DIVERSIFYING IS THE PROVERBIAL "DO NOT PUT ALL YOUR MACKERELS IN THE SAME BUCKET"

"Scaling in means investing little by little over a period of time to reduce the risk of poorly timing your purchases.

Look at what happened this morning. If you had bought Fat Fish stocks all at once yesterday, your wealth would be down by 20% today.

If you had scaled in and spread your purchase over the past month instead, you would have cushioned your loss: if you had bought half a month ago and half today, you'd be down 10% only.

The benefit of scaling in is that you average your purchase price. It reduces your downside risk.

In general, you could decide to scale in over any period of time: days, months, years, or even continually. The key is to stay disciplined about it.

You also wanted to learn about bonds?"

"Bonds sound less risky than stocks."

Castby nodded. "To some degree they are. Unlike stocks, bonds provide great visibility over future income. Clear as today's sky."

Catsby looked through the window. "You brought your swimsuit, right?"

As promised, Catsby invited Socrates on his boat. They took the rest of the day off. They sailed off the harbour and lazed around in the sun. It was way too warm to sight any penguins.

"Catsby, why are you called Catsby? You're a lion," Socrates asked.

"My adoptive family thought I was a cat when they found me, and I was rather flamboyant. Why are you called Socrates?"

"I had a different name at first. But then my parents figured I asked a lot of questions."

As the afternoon went, a strong wind rose from the shore. A bigger sail boat raced past, splashing water all over them as it powered ahead.

The playboy cat at the sail smirked while a cute molly cat at the back just ignored them.

"&$#@!" Socrates and Catsby exclaimed.

The fast boat got farther away. But suddenly, a strong wind broke the mast and swayed the ship. The boat capsized. They saw the two cats jump into the sea.

Catsby and Socrates rushed to get them out of the cold water. They pulled the cute molly cat onboard. "I'm Missy," she said as she climbed onboard shivering. The playboy was frozen and curled alone at the back.

When they reached the port, Missy kissed her saviours thank you and winked at Socrates.

Socrates discreetly asked her for her Catbot tag before she got into her sports car. She left her boyfriend wet on the quay.

Catsby and Socrates looked at each other. Catsby said: "Don't go after her. She will make you broke.

And come to my office tomorrow. We will talk about bonds. Strong bonds."

STRONG BONDS

BONDS

Catsby still had his sunglasses on. "Where did we leave off?"
he asked.

Socrates replied: "You said that bonds provide visibility over future
income, before we went sailing."

"Let's get back to our bonds then.

Bonds belong to a category of investments that financiers call 'fixed
income'. Investments in that category pay fixed amounts of money
to investors according to a fixed schedule. As a result, investing
in fixed-income products, and bonds specifically, is a great way of
earning predictable future income.

Do you remember what we said about the ways Fat Fish Company supported their business expansion?

One way the founders used to raise money was selling shares to stock investors. The other way was with debt.

Initially Fat Fish borrowed money from banks through loans. However, Fat Fish turned so successful and grew so large that even banks could no longer lend them the kind of money that they needed to keep on developing their operations.

So banks offered Fat Fish to help them raise a different kind of debt. They helped Fat Fish issue bonds.

If you remember, bonds are loans which are sliced into small pieces. So, when an investor purchases a bond, he simply owns a fraction of a bigger loan."

"I remember that."

"But you see, it is not just companies that borrow money this way. Governments also do."

"Really?"

"Absolutely. Sometimes the government of Catland takes loans from banks. Other times the government borrows money by issuing bonds."

"Why would Catland even borrow money?"

"Catland spends money on the running of the government, on roads, schools, hospitals... but they have limited sources of revenue.

For instance, the main source of revenue for Catland is the taxes that are collected from residents and businesses every year.

When tax receipts are too little to cover expenses and government projects, Catland borrows money, and they promise to repay it later with future tax receipts."

"Is there a difference between bonds from companies and bonds from governments?" Socrates asked.

"Bonds which countries issue are called government bonds, while bonds which companies issue are called corporate bonds. The names are different, but both work much the same way."

"Why are bonds safer than stocks?"

"We said that when an investor buys the stock of a company, he makes a bet on the future profits that the company will make. So in a sense, he buys hope.

But when an investor buys a bond, he buys something different: he buys a promise.

He is buying the promise that the company or the government which borrowed money will pay him back, with some interest on top. And bond issuers are bound by this promise: they have a bond.

Let's look at four new bonds that were issued in Catland last month.

Two of them were issued by the government, one by Fat Fish Company and one by Skinny Fish, Fat Fish's low-margin competitor.

Catland borrowed C$2 billion through two bonds. The first line was borrowing over 5 years: the government issued 10 million bonds, each worth C$100, with a maturity of 5 years and a coupon rate of 3.5%.

The second line was borrowing over 10 years: the government issued 10 million bonds, each worth C$100, with a maturity of 10 years and a higher coupon of 4%."

THE 4 FORMIDABLE BONDS

ISSUER	COUPON	MATURITY
🐾 CATLAND	3.5%	5 YEARS
🐾 CATLAND	4%	10 YEARS
🐟 FAT FISH	6%	5 YEARS
🐟 SKINNY FISH	9%	5 YEARS

"What does this mean for an investor who bought Catland bonds?"

"Each investor who bought Catland bonds gave $100 to the government for every bond they bought.

In exchange, Catland promised to pay each investor in a 5-year bond a 3.5% interest rate on $100, or $3.50, every year for 5 years, and to pay back $100 at the end.

Similarly, Catland promised investors in the 10-year bond to pay a 4% interest rate on $100, every year for 10 years, and return $100 after 10 years."

"What about the other two bonds?"

"Fat Fish issued a 5-year bond with a coupon of 6%, while Skinny Fish Company also issued a 5-year bond, but with a juicier coupon of 9%."

"Bonds seem to have clearly defined features," Socrates noticed.

"You are right. Unlike stocks, there is in principle little unknown about the payments that a bond will make.

When an investor buys a bond, he pretty much knows what he is going to get and when.

As you noticed, bonds have distinct characteristics:

– a redemption value, which is also called the principal of the bond. This is the amount of money that the borrower promises to repay the investor at the end.

– a maturity date, which is the date when the principal will be paid to the lender.

– a coupon, which is the interest rate that the bond will pay regularly to the lender, as a percentage of the principal.

– a coupon schedule, which spells out the dates at which interest payments will be made to the bondholder."

"That sounds neat. Are there a lot of bonds out there?"

"Stocks get most of the attention in the news. But the market for bonds is much larger. For one thing, bond markets include all the bonds that governments issue. This alone represents a fish load of money."

Socrates insisted: "So bonds really are safer than stocks?"

"If they are used well, they can be a relatively safe investment.

The clearly defined features of bonds are one reason why bonds are generally advertised as a great placement for investors looking for predictable, regular, recurring income.

But I will tell you something that financial advisers don't mention very often. Bonds are generally advertised as a safe investment. But the fact is that it is not entirely true."

"How so...?!"

"What is true is that when a company like Fat Fish issues both stocks and bonds, the bonds that the company issues are safer than its stocks.

The law protects bondholders more than shareholders: if Fat Fish ran out of cash, bankruptcy laws would make sure that lenders get paid before shareholders with whatever money the company has left."

"So lenders carry less financial risk than shareholders?"

"That's right. What is also true is that the bonds which governments issue are generally safer investments than the bonds which companies issue in the same currency.

WHAT A FAT FISH 5-YEAR BOND PROMISES TO PAY

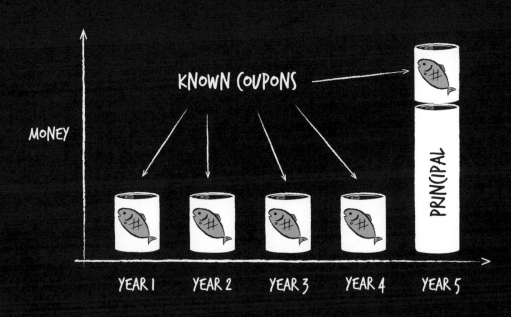

For instance, the bonds from the Catland government are generally safer than the bonds from Catland companies."

"Why is that?"

"Bonds are loans, right? Governments are quite likely to repay the money they borrow, when governments borrow in their own currency. After all, governments can sometimes print more of their own currency. They can also raise taxes in order to shore up deficits when there is a hole in public finances."

"So... how are bonds risky?"

"As always, it depends on who you lend to, and it depends on how long you lend for.

You need to remember this: bonds are a safe investment and offer a predictable return under two strong conditions only.

The first condition is that the government or the company issuing the bond does not default before the maturity date of the bond. Defaulting means stopping to pay.

The second condition is that the bondholder keeps the bond until its maturity and does not sell the bond early."

"So it is possible to sell a bond?" Socrates clarified.

"It is. Like other investments, you can sell a bond before its maturity.

But then, you have no guarantee of being able to sell a bond for the same price you bought it, or to recover the full repayment value that the bond represents."

Socrates squinted.

"Let me explain why the two strong conditions we just mentioned matter."

Catsby's phone rang. Catsby looked at the screen to check who was calling. He ignored the call and silenced the ringtone. He looked jittery though.

VOLATILE BONDS
BOND PRICES & YIELDS

"Like other investments, bonds carry risks," Catsby went on. "Should we sell a bond before its maturity date, we would find out that a bond behaves like a stock. Its price fluctuates.

It means that in some circumstances we could make a profit by selling a bond early. Other times though, we could only sell it at a lower price than we initially paid for."

"But... you said that bonds offered predictable income," Socrates said.

"Income, yes. Bonds do pay regular coupons at known dates.

What is unpredictable however is the resale value of the bond if the bond is sold early."

"What happens then?"

"You see, every bond has a price. And the price of a bond is expressed as a percentage of its redemption value, the amount of money that the borrower promises to pay back at maturity.

For instance, the 5-year-maturity bond that Catland issued last month promises to pay back C$100 after 5 years: C$100 is its redemption value. But C$100 is not always what a buyer would pay for the bond. The price will be determined by the market."

"Although you said that each investor who subscribed to Catland bonds at issuance gave $100 to the government for every bond they bought?"

"That's right. When a bond is first issued, it is generally issued at a price equal to its redemption value. So C$100 is the price at which the first bondholders bought the recently-issued Catland bonds. But if one of the first bondholders decided to sell a bond, the next investor would not necessarily pay C$100 for it. He might pay more, or less."

"Why is that? The bond still promises to repay the same $100 at the end," Socrates pointed out.

"Fair remark. But other factors matter too. I will explain why. Would you allow me to introduce the notion of 'yield' before that? It will help us understand why bond prices move.

When financiers talk about bonds, they do not talk about them in terms of price. Instead, they talk about returns. And the annual return of a bond is called the yield. OK?

The yield of a bond is the annual return that the bond promises to pay if the bondholder keeps the bond until maturity.

If you had bought the 5-year Catland bond at C$100 on the day it was issued, your yield would be 3.5%, the coupon rate. That's the annual return that you would get for owning the bond.

The reason why financiers prefer to talk in terms of yield rather than prices is because comparing the prices of two bonds is not straightforward. Every bond has slightly different features: different borrowers, different maturities, different coupons.

But yields make for an easy comparison between bonds. At a glance, anyone can compare how much various bonds promise to return. For the bonds we mentioned: it was 3.5% and 4% for Catland bonds against 6% for Fat Fish and 9% for Skinny Fish when they were first issued. Simple. Yields are a common feature across bonds. So comparing bond yields instead of bond prices is closer to comparing apples with apples."

Catsby carried on: "Now let's consider the issuance of a bond from the point of view of an investor.

When a bond is first issued, the yield of the bond, the return it promises, represents the interest rate that investors demand in order to lend money to the borrower until the bond matures."

Socrates thought for a moment. "So this means that when Catland issued a 5-year bond with a coupon of 3.5% last month, 3.5% was the interest rate at which, at that particular moment, investors were willing to lend to the government over 5 years?"

"Exactly right," Catsby said.

"And then what happens next?" Socrates asked.

"An investor could hold the bond and earn a 3.5% annual return until it matures. Or, if he decided to sell the bond, the investor would notice that the interest rate at which the government can borrow changes over time: interest rates reflect the price of money at which borrowers and lenders agree to do business.

Today for instance, investors would not lend to Catland over 5 years for 3.5% any more. Circumstances have changed and investors now have different anticipations about the future. They wouldn't lend unless the government paid a higher interest rate of 4%. So this week, when Catland issued a new 5-year bond, they issued it with a higher coupon of 4%."

"Did this new bond impact the old bond?"

"Let me ask you this question. Would you still want to buy an old Catland bond with a coupon of 3.5% at C$100 if you could get a comparable brand new Catland bond with a coupon of 4% for the same price?"

"No! I would prefer the bond with the higher return."

"So you would agree that the price of the 3.5%-coupon bond would need to drop to make the old bond attractive again? You wouldn't want to buy the 3.5%-coupon bond unless the old bond offered at least the same overall return as the new bond."

"Correct."

BOND PRICES FLUCTUATE...

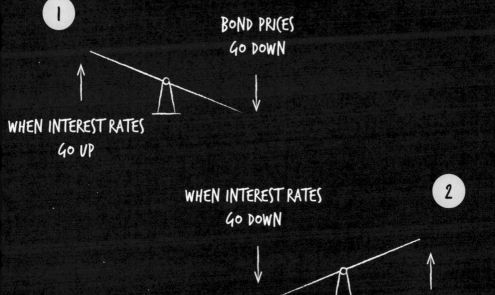

1

BOND PRICES
GO DOWN

WHEN INTEREST RATES
GO UP

WHEN INTEREST RATES
GO DOWN

2

BOND PRICES
GO UP

BOND PRICES & BOND YIELDS MOVE IN OPPOSITE DIRECTIONS

"And you would agree with me that the price of the 3.5% bond would need to adjust enough to make investors indifferent between buying the old 3.5%-coupon bond at a new lower price or the new 4% bond at $100."

"Makes sense."

"That's why bond prices fluctuate and a bond offers a predictable return only if an investor holds the bond to its maturity. In between the date of purchase and maturity, market conditions will affect the price."

"How about if a bond investor had to sell for unforeseen circumstances? Could he prepare for that?"

"A bond investor would need to be aware of something called the 'duration' of the bond he targets before he invests. Duration is an important property of bonds and a key risk measure for the prospective investor. Every bond has a specific duration."

Catsby's phone rang again. This time, the screen started flashing. He stared at it for a while. Then he silenced it again.

SENSITIVE BONDS

BOND DURATION

"Would you like some milk?" Catsby asked.

"I'd love some," Socrates replied. "Hm...," he said as he swilled his drink, "Isn't what you call 'duration' the same as maturity?"

"It is not. Duration is no doubt a confusing term. In the context of bonds, duration is somehow related to how long the maturity of a bond is. But specifically, the term 'duration' measures a kind of bond sensitivity.

Let me ask you a question before I tell you what it is exactly.

If I asked you to lend me a thousand dollars, would you accept to lend me at the same interest rate over 5 years and over 10 years?"

"No chance," Socrates said. "I would need to wait for an extra 5 years for you to repay me. I would request a higher interest rate to lend you for 10 years."

"That's fair. Generally, the longer investors lend money for, the higher interest rates borrowers have to pay."

Catsby started drawing on his notepad. He drew a curve that rose quickly at the beginning, then at a slower pace, before reaching a plateau. The vertical axis read "yield" and the horizontal axis read "maturity".

When he finished, Catsby said: "This is the ordinary shape of a bond yield curve. What it shows is that bonds with longer maturities tend to promise higher returns to investors.

It makes sense. Like you, the longer lenders part with their money, the more they ask to be compensated usually."

Socrates looked at the drawing: "I should buy the longest bond possible to get the highest return possible!"

Catsby acted cool. "Interesting..." he said. "Would you have bought the 5-year Catland bond with a coupon at 3.5% or the 10-year Catland bond with a coupon of 4% when they were issued last month?"

INVESTORS TEND TO EXPECT HIGHER RETURNS THE LONGER THEY LEND MONEY FOR...

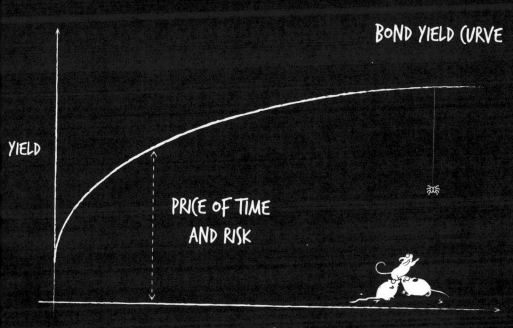

"The 10-year bond at 4%. It paid more," Socrates replied.

"On the face of it, it is tempting," Catsby said. "But there is a catch.

Higher yields are not free gifts. Higher returns tend to mean that investors are taking greater risks. Longer bonds generally promise higher interest rates. But the prices of longer bonds are also more sensitive to changes in yields. And duration measures how sensitive the price of a bond is to a change in the interest rates that investors request to lend. That's why investors should take duration into account.

Duration is a calculated number which gives an approximation of how many cents the price of a bond would drop or rise, every time the yield of a bond changes by as little as a percent of a percent (0.01%)."

"How would that apply to the Catland bonds?" Socrates asked.

"The 5-year Catland bond for instance currently has a duration of about 4. It means that when the yield of the bond changed from 3.50% to 3.51%, the price of the bond dropped by about 4 cents. And when the yield changed from 3.50% to 4%, the price dropped by about $2.

The 10-year Catland bond has a duration of about 8. So its price is twice as sensitive as the price of the 5-year bond. The price of the 10-year bond would drop twice as fast when yields rise."

"Oops... Is a higher duration always a bad thing?" Socrates asked.

"It depends. Do you remember how Missy's sailboat raced past us yesterday?" Catsby asked.

"Ah... Missy... Err... yes, my fur still has salt in it," Socrates babbled.

"The duration of a bond is a bit like the size of the sail on a boat.

Missy's boat had a bigger sail than ours. The bigger the sail, the more wind it catches.

When the wind is low, a larger sail helps a boat move faster.

But when the wind gets strong, a bigger sail gives too much traction. It can break a mast and sink a ship.

In that sense, a large sail on a boat is a double-edged sword.

A large duration does something similar for bonds. In the right conditions, it helps. Other times it hurts."

Catsby carried on: "A property of bonds is that longer bonds have longer durations: they are more sensitive to fluctuations in yields.

But it is not always a bad thing. The higher the duration of a bond, the faster the price of a bond rises when interest rates are falling. So a large duration makes a bondholder richer when interest rates drop.

But the higher the duration of a bond, the faster the price of a bond falls when interest rates go up. So a large duration hurts bondholders when yields rise.

Keep in mind that bond prices and interest rates move in opposite directions."

"So, owning bonds with a long duration makes sense when we anticipate interest rates to fall?" Socrates asked.

"That's right. And investing in bonds with a short duration is safer when we might need to sell our bonds early, or if we do not want to be exposed to a swift change in the interest rate environment."

"So it may not necessarily be a better idea to buy the 4%-coupon 10-year Catland bond compared to the 3.5%-coupon 5-year Catland bond?" Socrates asked eventually.

"Not necessarily. If you needed to sell your bond before maturity, then it would be open to debate.

Investors in the 10-year bond took twice as much interest rate risk for just a marginal 0.50% increment in their expected return. Maybe the extra risk is worth more than that."

Catsby's phone rang again. Only this time, it was flashing lights in all directions. Catsby sighed as he shook his mane. "Sorry, everyone's got a boss. I need to pick it up. My ex-wife's lawyer."

CAT ME IF YOU CAN

CREDIT RISK

"The lawyer says I still owe her money," Catsby said as he hung up. "Never ending... Anyway, there is one last thing I would like to tell you about bonds," Catsby said.

"What is it?"

"The risk of default. You might have experienced that, when we lend, we take the risk of the borrower defaulting on us. To default means to fail to pay."

Socrates told Catsby about Wily Cat, his street cat cousin, who never returned the C$1,000 Socrates lent him a year ago.

"Hm... painful," Catsby sympathised. "The probability that a borrower may default on their obligation to repay a debt is called the credit risk.

That probability is never zero. Even government bonds issued are not 100% safe. Sometimes even governments fail to pay back their debt. Look at the country of Miceland for instance. Their government is a disaster. They regularly fail to repay their bonds and leave their lenders broke."

"How do you assess the chance of a borrower not giving you your money back?"

"This is such a persistent problem that some organisations, called Rating Agencies, make it their full time job.

The main rating agency in Catland is Abnormal & Rich. Their job is to grade bonds that governments and companies issue. They rate issuers according to how worthy of lending they are.

In descending order, the marks they attribute range from investment grade, marks like AAA, AA, A, BBB, which mean a low chance of default, all the way down to junk, with grades like BB, B and CCC, which imply a high chance that lenders will never see their money again."

Socrates felt a shiver down his spine.

"Among the issuers of the four bonds launched last month, the government of Catland is currently rated AAA, Fat Fish Company is BBB, while Skinny Fish is only B. Not every bond is rated though."

"Is this why Catland could issue a 5-year bond with a coupon of 3.5%, while Fat Fish paid a higher interest rate of 6%, and Skinny Fish an even higher rate of 9%, all for the same 5-year maturity?"

"You get the drift. Lower ratings mean that issuers need to pay higher interest rates to persuade investors to lend.

Beside ratings, another way to assess credit risk is to look at how much a bond promises to pay on top of the return of a government bond with a similar maturity in the same currency. That difference is called the credit spread. It reflects the probability of default of the issuer.

For Fat Fish, the difference was 2.5% compared to Catland. For Skinny Fish, 5.5%. The higher the difference, the riskier the borrower. If a bond issuer could afford to pay lower interest rates, they would happily do so."

"So investors in the Skinny Fish bond get paid more... but they also take a greater risk of never seeing the money they initially invested?" Socrates asked.

Catsby nodded. "The reason why some investments offer higher returns is that they present greater risks.

Would you rather buy the 5-year Fat Fish bond with a coupon of 6% or the Skinny Fish bond with a coupon of 9%?"

"I'm not sure now."

"There is no clear answer. Your decision would be a trade-off. And implicit in the higher interest rate is the higher possibility of losing all the money you invested. On the flip side, if you manage to hold the Skinny Fish bond to maturity and Skinny Fish doesn't default, you would be able to earn the extra yield for the higher credit risk that you took."

Catsby summarised: "Bonds overall can be a great tool for visibility over future income if you know what to watch out for. But investing in a bond is not only about how nice a coupon it promises to pay. Bonds carry risks, and investors need to be aware of the kinds of risks they are taking. Among them: who the issuer is and how likely he is to default before maturity. How large the duration of a bond is and whether you will see rising or falling interest rates over the period of time you intend to hold the bond; and also, how liquid a bond is if you wished to sell it."

"Take your time to digest the information," Catsby said. "Call me when you are ready for our next appointment."

INTERMISSION:

THE FLAMING BORGHINI

The next morning, Socrates bumped into his neighbour, a sheep whom the kitties in the hood called Borghini.

Nobody was quite sure where Borghini came from or what his real name was. But he was known for running a nip joint, where he served the best moonshine in town. Regulars lovingly called it the catnip.

Borghini spoke with a lisp, and was smarter than he looked. "Socrates, I don't see you around anymore."

"Been busy going to the bank," Socrates replied.

"You too?" Borghini said.

"What do you mean?"

"I probably shouldn't mention. But keep it to yourself. I got a tip from your cousin Wily."

"Wily?" Socrates felt his fur rising. "Go ahead," he said.

Wily was a hustler after all. Who knew what he was up to these days?

"Wily let me in on some great property deals he's done lately."

"Like?"

"Listen carefully," Borghini said. "This is how he does it.

You know the *Stretch Times*, the weekend supplement of the *Black Cat Bone*? Wily screens their ads to look for houses.

Once he finds a target, he goes to the bank and gets the house valued. He gets a loan from the bank for 80% of the value of the house. So, say the bank values the house at C$100,000, Wily gets the bank to agree to grant him a loan for C$80,000.

Then he goes back to the house and negotiates the price down. He only buys it if he can get a 30% discount. So that's C$70,000."

"Right."

"Then Wily pulls a few favours. He gets his pals to refurbish the place with the extra C$10,000 that he got from the bank loan.

Once that's done, he goes back to see the bank. He tells them how the property looks brand new and is clearly worth more. Say C$120,000.

The bank says "OK" and revalues the loan. The loan gets topped up and revalued at 80% of the new property price estimate.

In the end, Wily paid C$80,000 for a house worth C$120,000. And he got it with a loan of C$96,000.

And you know what the best thing is Socrates? Wily put zero money of his own. Ze-ro."

"That sounds like Wily..." Socrates thought.

Borghini carried on: "Wily now rents out the place. He lives on the rent and the remaining C$16,000 that he got from the bank! Does it not sound like the dream...?"

"It sounds barely legal, yes," Socrates interjected. "Which bank even does that...?"

THE DODGY PROPERTY DEAL

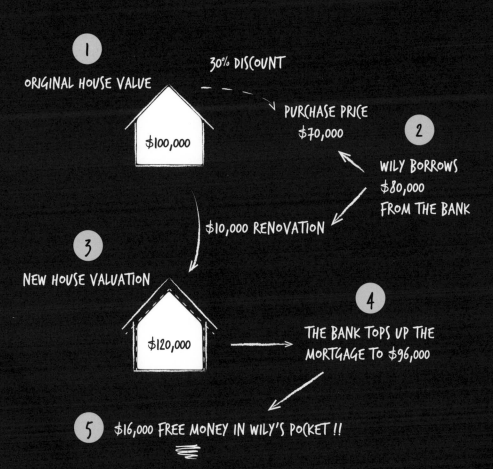

1 ORIGINAL HOUSE VALUE

30% DISCOUNT

$100,000

PURCHASE PRICE
$70,000

2

WILY BORROWS
$80,000
FROM THE BANK

$10,000 RENOVATION

3 NEW HOUSE VALUATION

$120,000

4

THE BANK TOPS UP THE
MORTGAGE TO $96,000

5 $16,000 FREE MONEY IN WILY'S POCKET !!

"Whatever. Wily's minted now! So I've been going to the bank quite a bit myself.

Dogland is booming. Banks from Dogland are expanding aggressively here in Catland. The bank I'm seeing is called Barks. I found a couple of promising properties and I'm getting my loans stamped."

"That sounds dodgy as fish... But thanks for the heads up, Borghini."

"Don't mention it!"

Socrates spent the rest of the day thinking about the property scheme. He wasn't sure what to make of it. At the same time, he could feel an itching temptation to know more...

MARGIN CALL

PROPERTY, LEVERAGE & BUFFER

"Back for more already?" Catsby said as Socrates came back to the bank offices.

"Well…" Socrates sighed, just before he spilled the beans over his neighbour's shady property deals.

"Interesting," Catsby said. "I think your neighbour doesn't have a clue what he's getting into.

But it's a great opportunity for us to speak about investments in property."

"How about my neighbour's deals?"

"Don't worry. We'll get to that shortly. Let's first understand how investing in property works, so you understand why what your neighbour and Wily are doing is dangerous.

Property has some interesting features. In previous meetings we spoke about stocks and bonds. And property is sort of a hybrid between bonds and stocks."

"How so?"

"Property, like bonds, can provide relatively predictable income in the form of rent.

Do you know what a rental yield is, Socrates?"

Socrates shook his head.

"The rental yield of a property is the ratio of the annual income from rent over the value of the property.

For instance, if a C$100,000 flat rented for C$350 a month, that would represent C$4,200 in income a year. So the rental yield of the flat would be 4,200 over 100,000, or 4.2%."

"It is like the coupon rate of a bond, or the dividend yield for a stock," Socrates noticed.

RENTAL YIELD

=

RENT

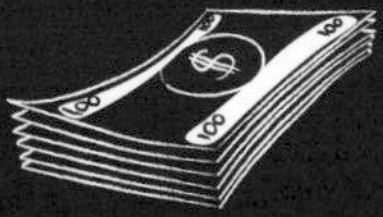

DIVIDED BY

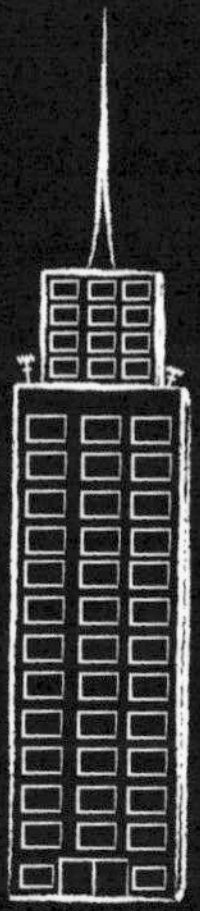

PROPERTY PRICE

"That's right. It is a measure of income," Catsby said.

"At the same time, investing in property is also very much like investing in stocks.

Properties, like stocks, do not have a fixed end date or a known future resale value. And investing in property is not just about collecting rent, but hopefully also about selling the property for a profit eventually.

So overall, property can offer both regular income and upside potential.

Now, an important practical distinction between stocks or bonds, and property is that property is one of the few assets that most cats can buy with a mortgage.

Most cats do not buy property entirely with their own money. They tend to also use money borrowed from the bank. A mortgage is effectively the use of debt. And that's perfectly acceptable.

But this is probably where your neighbour, Borghini, is confused. He does not take the full measure of the power of debt. Debt is not your money. It is money that you will have to repay later on, with interest."

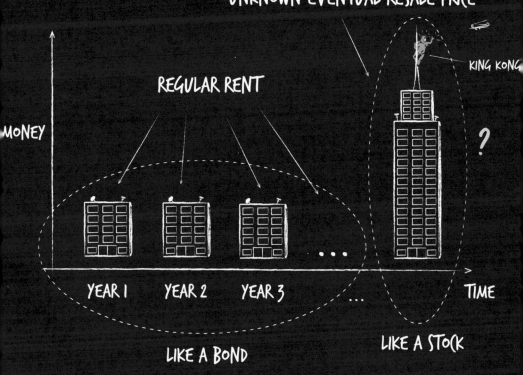

WHAT INVESTING IN PROPERTY LOOKS LIKE

UNKNOWN EVENTUAL RESALE PRICE

REGULAR RENT

KING KONG

MONEY

?

YEAR 1   YEAR 2   YEAR 3   ...   TIME

...

LIKE A BOND

LIKE A STOCK

"But you just said that taking a mortgage was perfectly acceptable…" Socrates said.

"Debt is not bad in itself. Debt is just a tool. Debt can be powerful, but it can also be dangerous."

Socrates moved away from the table.

"The most common reason why cats use debt is that it allows them to use money that they do not yet have.

But the reason why savvy investors find debt so compelling is that it magnifies the outcome of an investment. That's why debt is also sometimes called "leverage". Investing with leverage is like investing on steroids. When used skilfully, borrowing money to finance part of an investment can help increase its potential return. But leverage can also be dangerous, because it magnifies both gains and losses."

"How does it work?"

"Let's say that you purchased an apartment for C$100,000. A year later you manage to sell it for C$110,000.

If you completed the purchase 100% with your own money, you would make a C$10,000 profit over a year, or a 10% return on your initial investment."

"Right."

"If instead, you took a mortgage, say $50,000 at a 4% interest to help you finance the purchase of the apartment, you would only need to put in $50,000 of your own money.

When you sell the flat for C$110,000 after a year, you would repay the loan plus interest for C$52,000. You would then be left with $58,000, or an $8,000 profit. That would be a 16% return on your initial $50,000 investment, a pretty return, manufactured with the skilful use of debt."

"16% is sweeter than 10%!"

"Indeed. But wait a second. Let's consider a different scenario. Suppose that one year after the purchase, the property market dropped 10%, and you decide to sell the flat at a loss, for C$90,000 only.

If you had purchased the apartment entirely with your own money, you would lose $10,000, or 10% of your initial investment.

If you had purchased the apartment with the help of a $50,000 mortgage however, after the sale at $90,000, $52,000 would still go to repay the bank for the mortgage and interest. You would be left with only $38,000 from the sale.

You would have lost $12,000 on the $50,000 that you invested, or 24% of your initial investment.

If the price of the flat dropped 50%, then all the proceeds from the sale would go to repaying the bank and would leave you in debt.

When an investment makes money, leverage magnifies the profits. But, when an investment loses money, the loss becomes much greater than it would have been without leverage.

Debt is potent. It is not free money. If you intend use it, use it with caution."

Socrates Cat was stirred.

"Now, let's go back to your cousin," Catsby said.

"Wily spent $70,000 to acquire a property which is now supposedly worth $120,000. From a $96,000 loan, he spent C$10,000 on renovations and plans to spend the remaining C$16,000 on enjoying himself, right?"

"That's what Borghini said."

"Wily is making a number of mistakes.

LEVERAGE AMPLIFIES BOTH GAINS AND LOSSES...

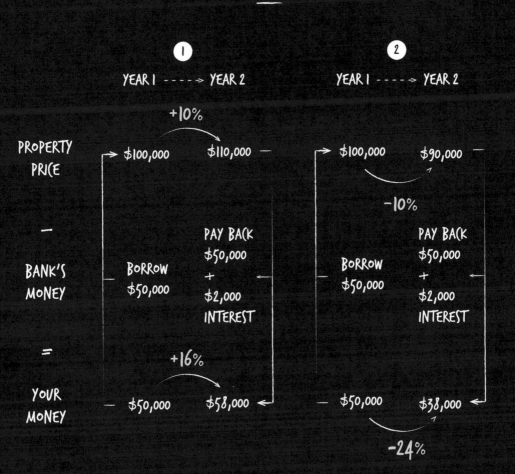

First, he is assuming the extra money that he borrowed from the bank and did not spend on the house is for him to spend leisurely, when in fact, none of the money that he borrowed is his yet. He still has to earn income from the property to repay his loan from the bank plus the interest.

Second, Wily may not have considered whether the rental yield of the property covers the cost of the loan. Given the amount of money that he borrowed as a proportion of the property value, your cousin hardly has any safety net if his tenant fails to pay rent one month.

Third, his underlying assumption is that the property market will keep going up."

Catsby took his notepad. "Let's look at the numbers.

Say that your cousin got the loan with an interest rate of 4% annually. On $96,000, that's $3,840 that he will have to pay every year on interest. That does not include paying back any of the money that the bank lent him in the first place.

Then, let's suppose that the rental yield on his property is 4%. On the $120,000 which the property is valued at, that's an annual rental income of $4,800.

Between his rental income and the interest payment, Wily would make less than $1,000 a year.

If the property market does go up a lot, this strategy may just work for your cousin, because a high appreciation in the property price may help him repay the loan once he sells the property.

If he is less lucky however, and the property market remains stable or goes down, his $1,000 annual income would take almost a century to repay the $96,000 loan that he took. And this assumes that Wily never misses receiving a single rent payment on his property."

"This does not leave him much room for manoeuvre..." Socrates reflected.

"Anyway, I suspect that his bank did not lend him money for 100 years. Wily will likely fail to repay the debt that he took on when the bank knocks on his door and the mortgage is due for repayment.

Wily might just end up bankrupt. His strategy is a typical case of being over-leveraged. And by the way, he's unlikely to ever return your $1,000."

Now Socrates was shaken.

"Debt can give the temporary illusion of wealth. But sometimes all that debt builds is a house of cards."

"You make it sound like debt is always bad?" Socrates said.

"It depends on how it is used. Debt can be a powerful enabler. If you use debt to start a project which is profitable enough to pay back debt over time, then borrowing can be a legitimate source of financing. But like in cooking, it is all a matter of proportions.

The distinction between good debt and bad debt is subtle because the problem is not with the debt itself. Debt is just a tool. It's how you use it.

It's also when you use it. There are times when taking on debt is less costly. Remember how we talked about the difference between apparent and real returns the second time we met?"

"You said that one had to take into account the effect of inflation in order to know one's real returns?" Socrates said.

"When you have debt, inflation is on your side. When you take on a fixed-rate mortgage, it is like issuing a bond yourself and promising to pay fixed coupons to the bank. In times of rising inflation, the value of the fixed coupons that you will pay to the bank, and even the value of the principal that you will return in the end diminishes over time, simply because the value of money depreciates.

So times of accelerating inflation favour borrowers who have taken a fixed-rate loan."

"Does this make me a sucker for renting at the moment?" Socrates asked. "The fast housing price appreciation of the past few years makes me wonder whether now is a good time to buy, or just wait."

"If you don't expect property prices to keep on rising in the near future, it is not a bad decision to rent in the current property market in Catland," Catsby said.

"The increase in property prices has slowed down in the past few months. Prices now seem to be stabilising or are on a slight downward path. Besides, rental yields in Catland are low nowadays: rents haven't caught up with how fast property prices went up in the past few years. Rental yields are around 4%, while the cost of a mortgage is also around 4%."

"So?"

"In a fast rising property market, it pays off to be an owner, because you get the benefit of the appreciation of the property price.

In a fast falling property market, it pays off to be a tenant, because you have none of the downside risk that an owner has to worry about.

In a stable or slowly declining property market as we are seeing now however, it's not clear-cut."

"What should you do then, in a stable market?"

"Consider that when you buy a property, all you do is transfer some money from your savings into an asset that you own.

So, supposing that the price of the property remains stable, you should be almost indifferent: you become no richer or poorer. Your savings are just allocated differently. Instead of having your savings in a liquid asset, something like cash or deposits at the bank, you have transferred wealth into an illiquid asset, the property. But the wealth is still yours. Do you agree?

But beyond the behaviour of the property market, two more elements come into the equation: income and mortgage.

When you invest in a property, income if any comes from rent. And the main cost is the mortgage. The difference between the rental yield and the mortgage rate is your financial buffer."

"How do you mean by financial buffer?"

"The difference between the rental yield and the mortgage rate measures how big a fall in the price of your property you can tolerate.

Suppose that you decided to buy a property, and you took a mortgage to pay for half the purchase.

Let's assume that the rental yield on the property is 4% and the cost of the mortgage is also 4%.

Since you took a mortgage on only 50% of the price of the property, then the cost of the mortgage also halved as a percentage of the property price. It would be 2% of the current price of the property, every year.

Between a rental yield of 4% and a cost of mortgage at 2% of the property price, the net income from the property is now 2% a year, right?"

There are two ways you can look at that 2% net income:

– You can see it as income for you to enjoy.

– Or you can see it as a buffer to protect you from a fall in property prices.

This 2% is your break-even point: as long as property prices fall by less than 2% a year, you would still make money from owning the property. If property prices fell faster than 2% a year however, you would be better off being a tenant."

"It's like thinking of rent as insurance," Socrates said.

"That's a good way to put it.

If the rental yield and mortgage cost numbers were different, the buffer would obviously look different.

What wouldn't change though is that you could still think of income as a form of cushion against capital losses. And this can provide a different perspective about when to buy and when to rent in a stable property market."

Socrates had come to the meeting with what seemed like a ready-made recipe for success. He now saw that there were more moving parts than he thought. And for all the appeal of shiny promises of return, it sometimes paid to be cautious.

DIAMONDS ARE FOREVER

FOREIGN EXCHANGE, COMMODITIES & ALTERNATIVE STORES OF VALUE

Socrates checked his news feed. Top of the list was "Dogland stock market up 30% year-to-date!"

Hopes for the economy of the neighbouring Dogland were running high. The aggressive lending by Dogland banks – like the Barks bank that Borghini mentioned – also betrayed the upbeat atmosphere that reigned on the other side of the border.

The news headline was a good enough reason to mention investing abroad at today's meeting with Catsby, and ask for his opinion. It was tempting to join the party...

"We haven't talked about investing abroad yet," Socrates said.

"You're thinking about Dogland?"

Socrates acted innocent.

"Investing abroad is no different from investing at home when it comes to the various asset classes which are available for you to invest in. There is one way in which it differs considerably though."

"What is it?"

"Foreign exchange. Remember when we talked about your base currency as we ran the test on the computer?"

"I do. I realise that investments in Dogland are in a different currency," Socrates said.

"It matters a lot. We need to pay great attention to the currency our investments are in. When we invest abroad, the first thing we invest in is not the investment itself. It is the currency in which the investment is denominated, even if we don't think about it."

"How is that?"

"I myself bought a property in Dogland. I was hoping for a stable or steadily appreciating investment.

Over the past year, the price of the property has remained stable. But the doglar appreciated 25% against the catdollar.

Although the value of the property in doglars hasn't changed, I potentially gained 25% on my investment, just on currency fluctuations."

"That sounds wonderful!" Socrates said.

"In this situation it is," Catsby replied. "But the mechanics work both ways. The price of the property could have remained stable, and the doglar depreciated.

Currencies are like the moving walkways on which we travel at the airport. The ground feels stable, but the conveyor belt keeps moving underneath.

So when we invest abroad, we need to weigh how the foreign currency may move compared to our home currency while we hold the investment. Currencies undergo fluctuations which significantly sway returns."

"What makes currencies fluctuate?" Socrates asked.

"In the short term, a lot of currency fluctuations is random noise: it is not exactly clear why they move.

However, over longer periods of time and intuitively, currency fluctuations tend to reflect the relative rate of returns that one economy offers over another.

You see, a currency appreciates when it is in demand. And a currency sees demand when people want to invest in the country of that currency, or consume the goods and services which that country produces.

Conversely, a currency depreciates when people want to get rid of it. It comes under selling pressure when people try to get their money out of the country, or they expect to achieve better returns on their money if they invest somewhere else.

So, the direction in which a currency moves over time reflects how attractive an economy is relative to other economies."

"How can you anticipate how attractive an economy is?" Socrates asked.

"It is an art more than a science," Catsby replied. "But investors look at various indicators which can point to trends.

How the difference between interest rates in different economies evolves can in some cases signal the relative strength of those economies.

The acceleration or deceleration of investment flows from foreign investors into the stock and bond markets of a country can be another indicator. The promise of better returns is a powerful magnet. Nimble investors try to capture a share of the anticipated economic growth abroad by buying foreign assets. The greater the promise, the stronger the magnet.

Eventually currencies adjust to reflect the relative strengthening of economies as money flows and finds a way to better returns."

"So should I buy a lot of doglars, or investments denominated in doglars at the moment?" Socrates asked.

"Great question. Do you think that Dogland currently has a stronger economy than Catland?" Catsby replied.

"It looks so. I heard it's easier to find jobs over there."

"Do you think Dogland will grow even faster?"

"I don't know. I haven't heard any news about that."

"Do you think that other people think like you?"

"I think so. It seems like the consensus view at the moment."

"Then the news is already in the price," Catsby said. "The current level of the exchange rate between catdollars and doglars likely already reflects the anticipated strength of the Dogland economy and the difference in growth speeds between Dogland and Catland.

The doglar could appreciate further if investors started to anticipate even faster economic growth in Dogland or a slowdown in growth in Catland.

Alternatively, we could see the doglar depreciate if growth in Dogland slowed compared to its anticipated pace, even if the Dogland economy kept growing at a brisk pace.

You see, absolute growth levels don't matter, it is all a question of acceleration and deceleration."

"All about expectations again...," Socrates said. "Is there another way that I could benefit from the growth of Dogland without making investments there directly?"

"There is. You could think about the things that Dogland consumes a lot of as a result of its rapid development.

For instance, the current growth in Dogland implies a greater need for raw materials, including construction materials, energy and food. The development of Dogland has caused an increase in the price of a number of commodities. If the economy of Dogland keeps growing at the current or a faster pace, that price increase may intensify."

"So a way of benefiting from the growth in Dogland could be to invest in the materials needed to fuel the development of the Dogland economy?"

"Indeed. Incidentally, this is also a possible rationale for investing in the commodities asset class.

An investor could buy raw materials like steel, wheat, oil, sand, if he expects that those materials and the things that are produced from them will see greater demand and become more valuable.

But keep in mind that, just like stocks, the direct link between changes in economic conditions and commodities makes commodity prices volatile. And a peculiar feature of commodities is that, unlike stocks, bonds or property, commodities generate no income. There is no buffer for changes in commodity prices."

"Nothing feels quite stable or safe," Socrates said.

"It is true that everything moves. Managing money is trying to solve a dynamic puzzle. Investors need to be one step ahead. But remember, even money in cash form is not stable."

"Yes, even the value of money changes and inflation can erode it," Socrates sighed.

"Since we are at it, there is something else that I would like to tell you about money.

The first time we met, we said that investing was about finding better stores of value than money for our wealth, in order to preserve or grow its value.

We also said that one risk to holding our wealth in cash is erosion from inflation. But there is another risk to holding money. The money that we use now has no value of its own."

"What do you mean?"

"The reason why we are able to use bank notes and credit cards to pay for toothpaste and rainbow shirts is because the government of Catland says that these kinds of money are legal ways of making payments. This is the only reason why everyone in Catland behaves as if catdollars were actually worth anything.

THE MONEY THAT WE USE NOW HAS
NO VALUE OF ITS OWN

But think about it, you can't do much with catdollars themselves. They do not look particularly nice, they taste of plastic, you can't eat them. That kind of money has a name."

"Money that looks ugly and tastes of plastic?"

"No, money whose value only relies on the faith of the people who use it. It is called 'fiat money'. Fiat money has got no value of its own. It is not like you could go see the authorities and ask them to exchange your catdollars against gold or anything else of value. Catdollars are a safe asset to hold only as long as it is possible to purchase things with them. And that is possible only as long as we and other cats trust the government and the institutions that mint money."

"Is this some kind of conspiracy theory?" Socrates asked.

Catsby laughed. "It's not.

The value of catdollars lies in your confidence that someone else will accept them as payment, and in your trust that the government of Catland will maintain their value over time.

But, as you have experienced with your cousin Wily, trust is a delicate thing, and there are many ways in which the value of catdollars could be tinkered with. If the government started printing too many catdollars, the catdollar would lose value for instance.

This sort of unusual considerations is why some investors like having contingency plans. And to be fair to them, there is a case for owning investments outside of the traditional financial system, because sometimes the system breaks down and the faith in the value of money disappears."

"What kind of investments are you thinking about?" Socrates asked.

A prudent investor will think about having some alternative stores of value. Alternative stores of value are valuable assets which are not stocks, bonds, property, currencies, or commodities, but instead things like fine art, antiques, collectibles, or precious metals like gold.

Like commodities, alternative stores of value generate no income. If anything they cost money to store."

"So why bother about them?" Socrates asked.

"You might have heard the recent news that a drool painting by Catson Pollock sold for C$140 million."

"I realise that it's possible to make money from these. But, like commodities, isn't the fact that they don't generate income a problem?"

"The absence of cash flow payments in alternative stores of value can actually be an interesting feature in the context of diversification. It means that those assets do not quite react to the same drivers as stocks, bonds and property. They do not derive their value from the same things. So we can't value gold or fine art the same way as we would value stocks.

We said that the price of a stock reflects the anticipations for the future dividends that a stock will pay. But the prices of gold and fine art are simply determined by how much demand and supply there is for them. Their price is simply a function of their real or perceived scarcity. That is not necessarily a superior valuation model. It is simply different. But different can be good, because different is the essence of diversification.

Another attractive feature of alternative stores of value such as fine art, collectibles, antiques and precious metals is that they have no counterparty risk, if you hold them yourself."

"What is counterparty risk?"

"When we buy stocks, or bonds, or simply when we have money at the bank… there is a chance, however slight, that the company or the government or the bank with which we have the contract might decline or fail to pay us what they owe. That is counterparty risk.

However, assets that we can hold ourselves do not have that problem. If you ever need them, you won't need to stand in line at the bank for them."

"Are you implying that I should buy and hold some gold then?" Socrates asked.

"It might be worth considering, although the reason for mentioning the benefits of alternative stores of value is not to make a particular recommendation. Instead, it is to highlight that various asset classes have different properties which can be desirable in different sets of circumstances."

"I realise that."

"If you do not wish to think of alternative stores of value as an investment, you can maybe think of them as a form of insurance. In times of crisis, the focus of investing shifts from growing wealth to preserving it. When it happens, it is important to have contingency plans and to own some investments which do not behave like everything else we have."

Socrates nodded.

Catsby pulled a folded document titled "The Building Blocks of an Investment Portfolio" out of his pocket and took a look. "We've got to the bottom of the asset class list!" he said. "Shall we meet after the weekend?"

INTERMISSION:

DOG DAY AFTERNOON

Socrates checked his Catbot over the weekend for a summary of the news.

The top news was the takeover of PiggyBank by Dogman Sacks, the largest bank in Dogland. The two banks were merging into a new company, PitBull Bank.

Socrates looked up more information on Poodle.com, the search engine. The comments on social media made it clear that it wasn't a friendly takeover.

So, when Socrates headed to his scheduled meeting with Catsby at the bank on Monday afternoon, his sixth sense warned him, he could smell something fishy.

Socrates presented himself at the reception: "I have a meeting with Mr Catsby."

"I'm sorry, Sir. We regret to inform you that Mr Catsby is no longer with us."

"How do you mean?"

"There's been some changes over the weekend, Sir. But I can see on the schedule that Mr Snoot Van der Kat will see you instead. He is waiting for you in Room 6."

Socrates wasn't happy. But he headed to the meeting room anyway. It was in the basement. He found Snoot, a panther, waiting for him. The room was bare. No windows, naked walls, a small table, two wooden chairs and a single light bulb.

"Hello Catfella," Van der Kat said, as he unbuttoned his jacket. "Close the door. Take a seat. Make yourself comfortable."

Socrates took a seat. But he wasn't comfortable.

"I went through your file. I wasn't impressed. It seems that not much work has been done since you first came to the bank a couple of weeks ago. So let's get going. I understand that you wanted to invest C$100,000, right?

It is your lucky day. I have exactly what you need." Snoot touched his belt and rubbed his paws.

"But..."

"Let me tell you about this incredible investment. It is an amazing product. The offer is only valid today. We might even run out of stock before we finish talking about it.

It is a 75-year note. It is principal-protected. It pays coupons indexed on the price of jellyfish as long as the ratio between the price of an ounce of gold and an ounce of silver stays below 81.

And 81... have you noticed? It's half the golden ratio. What's not to like about that? It's a once in a lifetime opportunity!"

"But..."

"Sign here."

Socrates hesitated.

Snoot pointed his claw at an empty space on the contract. "Here, above the line. Look, we don't have all day."

The fire alarm interrupted Van der Kat's sales offensive. "Hmm... fire drill. Stay here, fella. I'll be right back."

Socrates looked out the door. No one he knew in sight. So he took advantage of the chaos that the fire alarm had caused to wiggle his way out of the building.

He took a moment to calm down when he reached the street. He was dumbstruck. The meeting was a holdup... He had to talk to Catsby. But how to find him?

Socrates pulled his phone and asked the bot: "Search Catsby."

The bot replied: "One profile for Catsby on LeashedIn, the social clowder for professionals. Occupation: none. Previous gig: PiggyBank."

Socrates sighed in relief. "Send him a chat."

Catsby soon replied and offered to give Socrates a call. Socrates gladly accepted.

"Thank you for reaching out. I'm terribly sorry," Catsby said on the phone. "Our good old PiggyBank has been taken over by Dogman Sacks. It's a mess. There is fur everywhere. Their culture is so different. The new boss fired me like a stray cat. I'm a lion for fish sake! These Dogland banks... it's a dog-eat-dog world."

Socrates nodded in sympathy as he listened. He then told Catsby about what had happened over the meeting. The experience with the new adviser had been appalling. Socrates asked if Catsby would be able to help and keep on providing advice.

"I'm afraid that I'm no longer in a position to advise you," Catsby said.

"Even... informally? Please..."

On his phone screen, Catsby could see Socrates pulling a cute cat look. He sighed. "Just because it's you, Socrates. Meet me at the Clutter Café tomorrow 2pm."

And so they met at the terrace. Socrates ordered a cattuccino. Catsby was still in shock. He ordered a Catland Libre.

"I'm glad that you sneaked out of the meeting yesterday Socrates. Those people are bandits. You just learnt the hard way not to have blind trust in your financial advisers."

"Tell me about it... But why was Snoot so keen?!"

"You should always be aware of the incentives of your financial advisers. Financial advisers are often incentivised to place financial products. They get paid a commission when they manage to sell products. And they may have a stronger incentive to place complex products, because complex products pay higher commissions.

But you did well. Do not get into investments that you do not understand. They may promise higher returns than simpler products, but they may also have a lot of obscure conditions attached. Sometimes it is not quite clear how they work...

Besides, as you experienced, your financial advisers may no longer be around when you come back and look for them."

"I noticed that."

"I'm not saying that the product that Van der Kat pushed won't do well. I don't have a crystal ball. We just don't know yet.

However you have every right not to trust easily when you don't understand the risks that you are asked to take. If in doubt, take your time to think and make up your own mind. Once you sign in on a deal, you are on your own."

BE AWARE OF THE INCENTIVES OF YOUR FINANCIAL ADVISERS

"But where did this complex investment proposal come from? It is like nothing we discussed so far," Socrates said.

"There are varying levels of complexity in investments.

The investments that we talked about: stocks, fixed-coupon bonds, property, commodities... are the basic building blocks. But then some financial products combine them together or build upon them like layered wedding cakes."

"It felt like that."

"Bear in mind that banks are just intermediaries between those looking for financing and those able to provide financing. So banks act the same way as any other business. What they buy, they want to sell for a profit. They also try not to hold financial products for their own account for too long. It would be like Fat Fish Company storing up raw fish for no good reason.

Some of the financial products that banks end up holding are complex in nature. Some of these products are called derivatives. They are financial products which derive their value from the value of other financial products.

But banks do not always want to manage the risk of holding on to those complex products. Then they try to find someone else to take them over.

If banks can't get rid of them in their original form, what they might try and do is add a bit of lipstick to the product to make the bride look more pretty. This is where the magic world of structured products comes in.

Structured products can be a way for banks to recycle derivative positions that they no longer want to hold, but do not manage to sell either. Structured products are a bit like fish balls. For the consumer, it is not quite clear what ingredients are in it. The consumer might get quality fish if he's lucky. But he might also get second-rate tails and bones that didn't sell the previous day.

So be wary of complex products that you do not understand. It might be better to stay away than risk indigestion."

Socrates felt self-conscious asking this: "I realise that you no longer work for PiggyBank, but... have we covered everything that you wanted to tell me about how to manage my money?"

"I wish that we had spoken about a few more things, Socrates. I also wish that events had turned out differently."

"Does it mean that we won't meet again?" Socrates sobbed.

Catsby sighed. "I should probably finish what I started. Listen, how about we meet a couple more times, and we should be set. How does that sound?"

POOL THE WOOL

FUNDS

Socrates and Catsby met at the terrace of the Clutter Café again the next day. As Socrates looked around, the headline of the *Black Cat Bone* on the next table caught his attention:

"CAT40 up 7% since the Dogman and PiggyBank merger".

"What does that mean?" Socrates asked as he pointed towards the newspaper.

"It means that the news of the bank merger has probably buoyed Catland stocks.

Investors seem optimistic about the takeover. They expect the newly merged bank will reduce costs and make greater profits in the future.

This may also prelude further mergers in other sectors of the economy. So stock prices are up on average. They reflect upbeat investor anticipations."

"But what's the CAT40?" Socrates asked.

"Sorry. The CAT40 is an index of the 40 largest companies which are listed on the Catland stock exchange.

Overall, investors see the CAT40 as a relatively representative sample of the companies of Catland. So the index gives a sense of how the prices of stocks in Catland are moving overall.

For instance, before the merger, the old PiggyBank represented about 2% of the index, Cat & Pillar 3% and Fat Fish about 4%. Assuming that the 40 largest listed companies of Catland give a fair representation of the different sectors of the Catland economy, then the evolution of the CAT40 also gives a sense of where investors expect the Catland economy to be headed."

"Hm... that makes sense. If you don't mind, what were the other things that you wanted to tell me about?"

Catsby replied: "We covered the building blocks of an investment porttfolio: cash, stocks, bonds, property, the influence of foreign exchange, commodities and alternative stores of value, as well as a number of risks to take into consideration when investing.

But there is a practical investment vehicle that we haven't talked about yet. Now is the time to talk about funds."

"Funds... what are they?"

"A fund is simply a basket of various investments, which is managed by a professional money manager.

You should now have a better understanding of how investments in various asset classes work. But if you do not yet feel comfortable with picking individual stocks, bonds, properties or commodities yourself, you don't have to. You may, but you also have alternatives: you can get investment professionals to help you make that selection and manage the selection for you over time."

"How could I get professional help?"

"One way of getting that selection made for you is by investing in funds. Investing in a fund is effectively hiring someone to manage a sum of money for you.

The way a fund works is that it pools money from various investors together. A money manager then invests that pool of money with the objective of producing income or capital gains for the investors in the fund."

"Does it mean that the money manager can do whatever he wants with the money?"

"He can't. The money is managed according to a specific mandate, whose investment objectives and limits are stated in the documentation of the fund.

You would choose a fund based on which asset class it invests in: stocks, bonds, property, commodities or a mix of those. But you would also choose the fund based on the investment strategy that the fund adopts: whether it focuses on income, growth, particular subsections of the asset class...

For example, a possible mandate for a fund which invests in stocks could be to invest in the stocks of mature companies in Catland within the hotel and leisure industry."

"I see."

"The convenient thing about funds is that they are baskets of investments. So by construction, they provide some diversification, within one particular asset class, or across various asset classes."

"Is there a catch?" Socrates asked.

"The downside of investing in a fund is that fund managers charge fees for their services."

"How much do they charge?"

"It depends on the fund," Catsby said. "There are two broad categories of funds: indexed funds and actively managed funds. The fees can range from just a few basis points, which means a few percents of a percent, of the money managed annually in the case of indexed funds, to several percents of the money managed annually for active funds."

"What is the difference between indexed funds and active funds?" Socrates asked.

"In an actively managed fund, the fund manager selects investments and adjusts his selection over time according to his best judgment and within the limits prescribed by the mandate of the fund.

This way, the fund manager strives to generate a better

performance than the average return of the market in which the fund invests. This is also why you would pay them higher fees: you would expect active managers to add insight and value."

"How about indexed funds?"

"In an indexed fund however, the fund manager has no discretion over the selection of investments within the portfolio.

Index funds are also called tracker funds. A tracker fund aims to replicate the performance of a particular market.

An example of a tracker fund could be tracking the performance of the CAT40 stock index."

"How would it do that?"

"The tracker fund would purchase each component of the index according to its respective weight in the index.

For instance, the old PiggyBank represented about 2% of the CAT40 index before the merger, Cat & Pillar 3% and Fat Fish company about 4%. So for every C$100 that an investor would place in a CAT40 tracker fund, C$2 would have been invested in shares of the PiggyBank, C$3 in Cat & Pillar and C$4 in Fat Fish, and similarly in the stocks of the other companies that make the CAT40 index."

"Are indexed funds just for stocks?"

"Tracker funds are not limited to stock markets. There can be tracker funds for government bonds, or corporate bonds, property, commodities... where the funds replicate specific bond, property or commodity indices."

"That seems handy," Socrates said.

"It can certainly make life easier.

What you would need to know though is that, in a tracker fund, the money will be invested with no consideration for the quality or the purchase price of the underlying investments, as long as they are part of the index to track.

In an actively managed fund however, the fund management team may choose only the individual stocks, or bonds, or property investments which they believe are good investments.

For example, the manager of an active fund whose mandate is to invest in Catland stocks may decide to invest in only 10 of the 40 stocks that make the CAT40 and maybe in some other stocks outside of the CAT40 index that they feel are worth buying. Active funds have more discretion."

"But they charge higher fees," Socrates pointed out.

"That's right. That's why some investors prefer investing in a tracker fund instead. It is a cheap and simple form of diversification.

If, for instance, all you aim for is to return the performance of the Catland stock index, you could invest in a tracker.

Investing in indexed funds is a form of passive replication and is sometimes referred to as 'tracking beta'. In financial jargon, tracking beta is another way of saying 'following the market'.

Active investing however looks to generate 'alpha', or extra performance."

"I'm an alpha cat! Alpha cats stick their necks out, while beta cats follow," Socrates thought as a way to remember.

"Some investors believe in the value and expertise that an active fund manager may provide, as they think that active fund managers may spot distortions in prices, anticipate events better and take advantage of those insights to do better than just passively tracking the performance of a market."

"You make me think of music," Socrates said.

Surprised, Catsby asked: "How so?"

"As you describe the two approaches to investing, I am thinking that... in the passive approach to investing, you track the performance of a market without making judgments. In a sense, it is like listening to music and letting yourself go with the musical flow.

In the active approach to investing though, it is like listening to music while remaining attentive to possible dissonance."

"You are right Socrates. When the prices of different investments tell a consistent story, they form a kind of harmony.

But when prices appear out of tune, the tension can be a sign of an impending danger or an opportunity. And active managers can decide to act accordingly."

"Which approach do you think is best, Catsby?"

"Both approaches have their merits and the jury is out.

Some actively managed funds return fabulous performances, while the performance of many other actively managed funds do not even match the performance of simple indexed funds consistently. So it is legitimate to ask how can those underperforming actively managed funds justify the more expensive fees they charge?

Finding an outstanding portfolio manager is no easy task. So, if you were to decide to go down the route of investing money through actively managed funds, you should be careful how you select the fund manager."

"How could I assess a fund manager before investing?" Socrates asked.

"You are raising an important question.

To measure the performance of fund managers, we first need to define what to measure them against. And to answer this question, we will need to talk about the objectives of active fund managers.

Actively managed funds target one of two types of performance: they either target absolute performance or relative performance."

"What is the difference?"

"Funds with an absolute performance target want to make money and generate positive returns, whether or not the markets in which they invest go up or down.

The first part of assessing the performance of these funds is relatively straightforward: you see whether they made or lost money.

But that's not all: the more difficult part is getting a sense of how much risk the funds had to take in order to generate their results.

One measure to gauge this is the Sharpe ratio. But there are other similar metrics. The Sharpe ratio measures how much the fund returned above the risk-free rate, the return that an investor could get from very short-dated government bonds, for the amount of risk that the fund took.

So the Sharpe ratio is the ratio between the extra return that the fund generated and how volatile the underlying investments were. The higher the ratio, the better the skills of the fund manager.

A Sharpe ratio below 1 is not good enough. A Sharpe ratio above 2 is very good. A Sharpe ratio greater than 3 is considered excellent."

"How about relative performance?"

"Other funds aim for relative performance. What this means is that they measure their investment performance against the performance of a reference portfolio called a benchmark.

A benchmark is like the CAT40 index: it is a model portfolio which mimics the overall performance of a particular market or an asset class. The performance of the benchmark, positive or negative, sets

SHARPE RATIO

=

FUND PERFORMANCE / DIVIDED BY

VOLATILITY OF RETURN

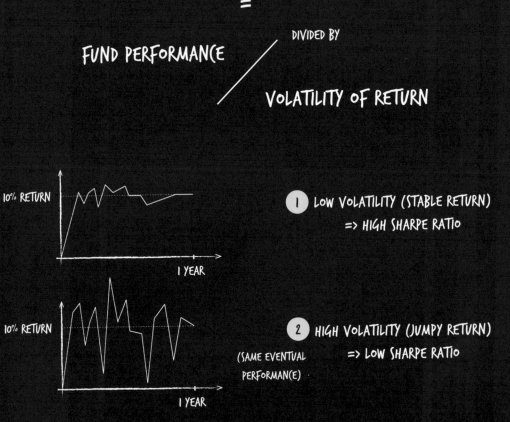

1 LOW VOLATILITY (STABLE RETURN)
=> HIGH SHARPE RATIO

2 HIGH VOLATILITY (JUMPY RETURN)
=> LOW SHARPE RATIO

(SAME EVENTUAL PERFORMANCE)

10% RETURN

1 YEAR

10% RETURN

1 YEAR

the performance that the fund manager has to exceed."

"Would you have an example?"

"Let's say that you decided to invest in a fund benchmarked against the CAT40 stock index.

If the CAT40 index was up 10% at the end of the year, and the fund returned 8%, the return of the fund would not qualify as a good enough performance, even if it is positive. A good performance should be above 10%, the return of the benchmark.

If instead the CAT40 index declined 10%, but the portfolio manager lost 8%, the negative performance would qualify as a decent return in the context of relative performance funds. The fund manager did manage to do better than the benchmark."

"So even losing money could be considered a good performance?"

"That's right. In the case of a relative performance fund, it could. But just like for active funds, you would also need to pay attention to the risk that the fund manager took. The equivalent of the Sharpe ratio for a relative performance fund is called the information ratio. It is the ratio between the fund returns over the benchmark and how volatile the underlying investments were.

Now we can answer your question: 'How do I choose an actively managed fund?' Here is a checklist of several questions you need to ask.

1. Exposure:
Does the fund provide exposure to the asset class or to the sectors of the economy that you would like to have exposure to?

2. Past performance:
Is the fund manager good? Past performance is obviously no guarantee of future performance, as the circumstances of the past may not repeat themselves. That being said, the 'track record' of the fund, how the fund's past performance compares with the past performance of the benchmark, is unfortunately often one of the few measures that you can check to assess how skilled a fund manager is. So do take a look at their track record. If it's not good, why go any further?

3. Risk:
Do not be blinded by past high performance or the promise of high returns. Actually, do not just focus on performance alone. Safeguarding your money should be high on your mind. So make sure that you are comfortable with the investment philosophy and investment process of the fund. In other words, is the fund manager

CHOOSING A FUND CHECKLIST

- ☑ RIGHT EXPOSURE
- ☑ PAST PERFORMANCE
- ☑ APPROPRIATE RISK
- ☑ LIQUIDITY

GIVING YOUR MONEY TO SOMEONE ELSE TO MANAGE IS A BIG DECISION.
ASK QUESTIONS, IT IS YOUR MONEY. IF IN DOUBT, STAY AWAY.

trying to generate the returns that you are looking for in ways that you are comfortable with? It is important to understand how the portfolio manager achieves his returns and whether he generates his performance based on his good judgment or just reckless gambling. You need to be satisfied with how robust and consistent the investment process is.

4. Liquidity:
How liquid is the fund? How easy would it be to get your money out of the fund if you decided to get your money back?"

"What if the managers say that they are good?" Socrates asked.

"They will always do... But giving your money to someone else to manage is a big decision. Do not be intimidated by authority. Ask questions, it is your money. You have every right to know how it will be managed. If in doubt, stay away."

Socrates summarised: "What you said is that, instead of buying individual stocks and bonds, properties or commodities, I could invest in various funds to have access to different asset classes?"

"That's right. Bear in mind that you don't need to go through a bank to invest in a fund. You can approach a fund manager directly.

You can also go through online fund platforms and shop for better funds. Or you can even use robo-advisers."

"But how would I decide to allocate money across various asset classes?" Socrates asked.

The sky had become overcast and a chilly breeze started blowing. "How timely," Catsby said. "The weather is changing. I will answer your question tomorrow if that's OK, Socrates. We will talk about economic seasons."

ANY WAY THE WIND BLOWS

ECONOMIC SEASONS

It was raining mice and rats outside. Socrates and Catsby met inside the café. Catbsy was reading the *Black Cat Bone* when Socrates arrived. The front page of the paper read "Dogland central bank cuts base rates by 0.5% as growth falters".

Socrates looked through the window obscured by rain drops and asked: "Today we'll talk about... the weather?"

Catsby folded the paper and replied: "Yes, we will talk about seasons. You see Socrates, most cats think about investments simply as ways to make money. But few cats see investments as tools."

"But they are ways to make money," Socrates countered.

"They are. But what most cats forget when choosing investments is how important the circumstances are for an investment of a particular type to do well.

Stocks do not do well in the same circumstances as bonds; and bonds do not do well in the same conditions as commodities.

Different asset classes are sensitive to different things."

"So you're saying that before selecting particular investments, we should also think about what we expect the future to be like?"

"That's right. And more precisely, we should think about what economic conditions we expect.

While you could obsess about one particular asset class – stocks, bonds, property, commodities, etc. – and how to juice returns out of it, you could also take a step back and think about why you are choosing this particular asset class at this particular moment in time.

You see, when it's winter, we do not wear the same clothes outside as when it's spring. Likewise, different investments are tools to prepare for different types of anticipated economic circumstances, the future economic weather so to speak."

"But you could still focus on finding good deals within a particular asset class?" Socrates pointed out.

"You are right, you could do that. A particular investment within an asset class may have its individual merits.

For example, a specific property in town may have great appreciation potential as a result of a new underground train station being built nearby. Or the stock of Skinny Fish Company may currently be undervalued compared to Fat Fish Company.

However, that property will not be entirely insulated from what the rest of the property market does, just like the stock of Skinny Fish Company will not be immune to how the rest of the stock market performs.

If the property market or the stock market were to move in one direction as a whole, the price of this particular property or of the Skinny Fish stock would likely be impacted as well.

That's why investments also need to be considered in the broader context of their own market and in the broader context of the economy."

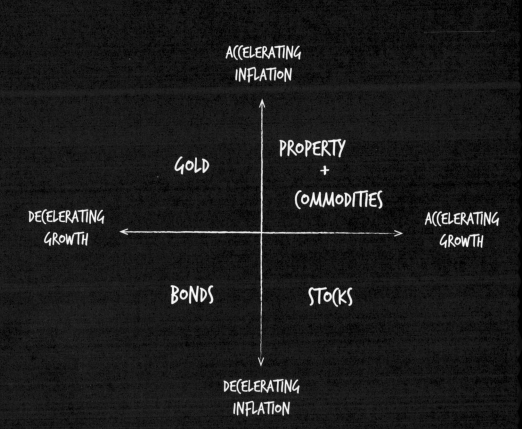

"So how do I look at... the economic weather?"

Catsby unfolded a napkin and he started drawing a quadrant.

"We could define four economic seasons, where each season reflects the four possible combinations of both rising and falling inflation and rising and falling economic growth.

"Why do you call them seasons?" Socrates asked.

"Because the different combinations tend to come back with a certain regularity as the economy ebbs and flows."

"And why inflation and economic growth?" Socrates carried on.

"These two variables in particular are important measures for taking the pulse of the economy. They are important at least for two reasons.

First, because the various combinations of these two variables dictate the real return of the economy as a whole, which then trickles down into the returns that different types of investments capture: dividends for stocks, coupons for bonds, rent for property and the evolution of the prices of raw materials.

Second, because the various combinations of these two variables influence the behaviour of a powerful actor in the economy:

the central bank. Inflation and economic growth happen to be the two obsessions of the central bank."

"The central bank? I don't think that you told me about them before... but I saw them mentioned in your newspaper today. What do they do?"

"Each country has a central bank.

The central bank is the state monopoly in charge of monetary policy."

"What is monetary policy?" Socrates asked.

"The purpose of monetary policy is to support economic growth and to keep prices rising, but not too fast, by regulating the amount of money in circulation in the economy. Let me break down that sentence," Catsby said.

"Please."

"Supporting growth should be a relatively straightforward goal to understand."

"I think so," Socrates said. "I can see why we should care about growth. It is important to create new jobs; and growth, at least in theory, is supposed to help the people of Catland become more prosperous. But what about keeping prices rising?" Socrates asked. "You said that inflation was bad."

"The first time we met, we explained why inflation was the enemy of savers. But a bit of inflation is actually good for the functioning of the economy."

"How can it be? It makes savers poorer!" Socrates said.

"Precisely," Catsby replied.

"In a consumer-led model of economic growth as we have in countries like Catland or Dogland, a bit of increase in the prices of goods and services supports economic growth.

Think about it, rising prices incentivise consumers to buy now. If prices are expected to rise in the future, it creates a sense of urgency. It makes sense to buy things today before they get more expensive tomorrow."

"That's evil!" Socrates said.

"A little bit. But it is all a matter of dosage, because too much inflation is harmful.

When inflation runs too fast, cats lose purchasing power too quickly, life becomes unaffordable, and businesses cannot adjust their prices fast enough to pass on their rising costs of operation, so their profit margins deteriorate and some companies end up going out of business."

"That sounds awful."

Catsby carried on: "Strangely enough, the other extreme, negative inflation, which we also call deflation, is just as bad for the economy as too much inflation.

Cats stop buying as they realise that there is no hurry to go shopping. They can afford to delay their consumption as they get better deals the longer they wait!

This may be good for consumers temporarily, but it is terrible for companies and the cats they employ."

"Oh yeah."

"That's why a lot of central banks, not just the central bank of Catland, want to achieve a bit of inflation, say 2 to 3%, in their economy every year.

If the general level of prices in their economy doesn't go up, central banks will work to engineer some inflation. But if inflation runs too fast, central banks will fight it.

So a central banker's dream for inflation is the story of Goldilocks and the bears: not too hot, not too cold."

"I think I get the picture. But what does the amount of money in circulation in the economy have to do with these growth and inflation objectives?"

"The central bank influences economic growth and inflation by stimulating or cooling down demand. And the main tool that the central bank uses to influence the level of demand is tweaking the cost of borrowing money. They make borrowing more or less expensive."

"How do they do that?"

"The central bank generally adjusts the cost of money by setting and adjusting the level of very short-term interest rates; it sets the cost of borrowing money over very short periods of time."

"Could I borrow from the central bank?" Socrates asked.

"You couldn't personally. But regular commercial banks do, and then in turn you would borrow from regular commercial banks. So when the central bank lowers short-term interest rates, borrowing indirectly becomes cheaper for every cat as well.

Cheaper borrowing stimulates consumption, as cats take loans and spend more. This is what the central bank does when they notice that demand becomes too weak to absorb what companies produce."

"Is that what the newspaper was referring to today?"

"Yes, the central bank of Dogland reduced the level of short-term interest rates to stimulate demand and cushion the slow-down that they now anticipate in their economy."

"Does a central bank only lower rates?" Socrates asked.

"No, they also raise rates when necessary.

When the central bank raises short-term interest rates, it makes borrowing more expensive. When borrowing money becomes expensive, cats reduce their spending, as they focus on repaying the money that they already owe instead.

This is what the central bank does when they anticipate that demand comes close to matching the capacity of production of the economy and overheating demand starts producing more inflation."

"I see."

"So all in all, what the Catland central bank does on average is encouraging cats to borrow money at just the right pace so the economy keeps on expanding at a nice rhythm.

In a demand-driven model of growth as we have in Catland or Dogland, debt is the fuel that the central bank relies on to adjust the temperature of the economy."

"So cats are encouraged to take on debt?"

"Somehow they are. This is how our current economic system is designed to work."

"Just so that central banks are in a position to engineer growth and inflation as they please?" Socrates asked.

"Central banks are not all powerful. They do not quite engineer growth and inflation at will. But they certainly have tools to influence these two variables.

Bear in mind though, the central bank does not ordinarily control longer interest rates. Longer interest rates tend to be

2 WAYS THE ECONOMY INFLUENCES THE PRICES OF INVESTMENTS

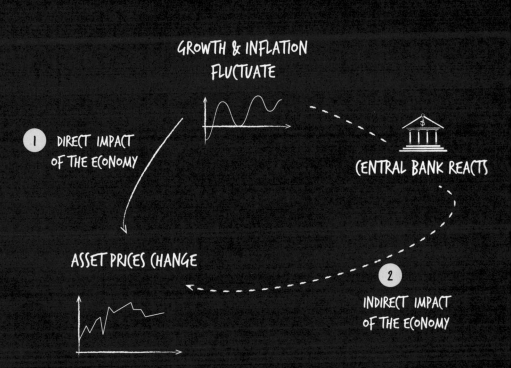

GROWTH & INFLATION FLUCTUATE

1 DIRECT IMPACT OF THE ECONOMY

CENTRAL BANK REACTS

ASSET PRICES CHANGE

2 INDIRECT IMPACT OF THE ECONOMY

determined by the borrowing and lending activity of companies, the government and individuals.

But once the central bank sets the level of short-term interest rates, this somehow percolates to interest rates for longer borrowing maturities.

Through monetary policy, the central bank sets the general tone for interest rates."

"Like a conductor trying to set the tempo?" Socrates asked.

"In a way, yes, and when the central bank of Catland or Dogland sets the level of short-term interest rates, it influences the heartbeat and the trajectory of their economies."

"I see. But back to the beginning of our conversation, how is the central bank relevant to my investments?" Socrates asked.

"The various combinations of economic growth and inflation influence the direction in which the central bank changes short-term interest rates. And as the central bank changes the level of short-term interest rates, it also affects the value of investments."

"How would short-term interest rates affect my investments?"

"For bonds, the answer should be reasonably straightforward.

The prevailing level of interest rates affects the return that investors demand when they lend money out. So it affects the yield of bonds, which is the return that investors request to lend to governments and companies.

So when the general level of interest rates changes in the economy, the prices of bonds also change.

When economic growth and inflation slow down, central banks are more likely to intervene and lower interest rates to stimulate the economy. When interest rates are expected to fall, the prices of bonds go up.

Conversely, bonds perform poorly in an environment of overheating growth and rising inflation. First, because central banks are likely to raise interest rates to cool down demand and the pace of inflation, and the prices of bonds go down when interest rates are expected to rise.

Second, because bonds see the real value of their future fixed payments eroded by fast inflation if the central bank fails to keep inflation in check."

"I see how central banks can affect bond prices. How about stocks?"

"For stocks, the link is a little more subtle, but still real.

Collectively as an asset class, stocks tend to perform well when economic growth is expected to improve. The underlying assumption is that companies will be able to reap the benefits of accelerating growth: consumers will get richer and will buy more products.

When central banks adjust the level of interest rates, they influence the trajectory of growth in the economy, so they also steer the future profits of companies.

However something more subtle also happens in the process. If you remember, when we spoke about stocks the day the locksmith blew the door, we said that the price of a stock reflects the value of the company's future profits. But because time is money, far away profits are less valuable than close profits. Profits in the distant future need to be depreciated compared to earlier ones to reflect their diminished value."

"I remember this," Socrates said.

"Interest rates measure the price of time. They represent the returns that investors request over different time horizons.

So the higher the prevailing interest rates, the higher the price of time, and the more we need to depreciate distant anticipated profits when we assess the fair price of a stock.

That is why, all future anticipated dividends being equal, higher interest rates weigh on stock prices. And vice versa, lower interest rates bolster stock prices.

Stocks are not just sensitive to the future profits of companies. They are also sensitive to the interest rate environment."

"I get the idea," Socrates said.

"The reason why it is important to have notions about how monetary policy works is this: we can understand a lot about how the price of certain assets react to news, events and economic data when we have a sense of what the central bank will try to achieve as a consequence. Central banks influence interest rates, which in turn impact the prices of assets."

"And investing is about being one step ahead," Socrates added.

"Investing is all about anticipations. So part of the game for investors is to assess how the central bank may adjust interest rates next, as economic conditions evolve."

"How about property?" Socrates asked.

"Property is interesting. Look at the quadrant. Different dynamics are at play.

The level of interest rates affects the cost of mortgages. Lower interest rates mean cheaper access to housing. But interestingly, the times when interest rates tend to fall, under the influence of the central bank, is when economic growth is slowing down. This also corresponds to times when people feel less wealthy to buy a property.

So on balance, property prices do not benefit from falling interest rates as much as they do from an expanding economy and a strong employment environment, when cats tend to feel richer and allocate money to buying property or can afford to pay higher rent. Property can also do well in times of accelerating inflation, when investors may see investing in bricks and mortar as a safer store of value than holding money, and the rising cost of construction materials makes existing properties comparatively more attractive."

"Commodities?"

"The prices of commodities tend to correlate with the economic cycle. For instance, the recent fast economic growth in Dogland stimulated demand for raw materials, and exacerbated their relative scarcity when production did not follow.

The prices of commodities also tend to rise in times of inflation, especially when inflation results from strong demand for raw materials, or higher energy prices. An important component in the price of commodities is indeed the energy consumed in extracting, producing and transporting commodities from the place where they are sourced to the place where they are used."

"Did you mention alternative stores of value?"

"Alternative stores of value tend to appreciate in extreme times.

Their price tends to rise when the economy is racing forward and there is excess money looking for a home. Think about how tycoons bid for art in times of economic euphoria.

Alternatively the prices of alternative stores of value can rise when investors seek ways of protecting their wealth in times of great uncertainty, be it under the threat of inflation, or when trust in political and financial institutions is weak, and the faith in the value of money evaporates. Unlike money, gold for instance exists in limited quantity. That gives it value."

Socrates looked at the drawing Catsby had made on the napkin. "So it does seem like different asset classes react to different types of economic circumstances."

"The season quadrant also illustrates why correlations between different asset classes seem like they change over time.

For instance, we sometimes hear the misconception that the prices of stocks and bonds should move in opposite directions: when stock prices go up, bond prices supposedly go down. But we often observe that this is not a consistent relationship.

Correlations between asset classes are not stable over time. But this is not because the correlation between two supposedly correlated asset classes breaks down all of a sudden. Asset classes are not correlated to one another to start with.

Instead they are correlated to the underlying economic conditions. And when underlying economic conditions change, different asset classes respond to those new conditions differently.

That is why a key to choosing your asset allocation is understanding the kind of environment in which particular asset classes do well."

"So what asset allocation is appropriate right now?"

"You see Socrates, the seasons are not about currently prevailing economic conditions; they are not about the current mix of growth and inflation. The seasons are about the expectations of acceleration and deceleration of inflation and growth. Again, it is about anticipations.

So there are two possible scenarios: either we have a good sense of what is going to happen next − in this case we can choose investments among the asset classes that we expect will tend to perform best; or we humbly confess that we don't know − in that case we need to diversify."

Catsby gave the napkin to Socrates. "Shall we meet one last time tomorrow?"

KILL BILLS

FEES & DEFLATION

Socrates was already in the café when Catsby arrived. Catsby apologised for his delay: "I'm sorry, I'm trying to cut my expenses. I walked today."

"Please don't apologise."

"We have covered a lot of ground," Catsby said as he pulled a chair. "You would have realised by now that my goal was not to dictate what to do with the money you inherited. Instead our conversation should have given you a simple framework, so you can ask yourself and your advisers the right questions in order to make better investment decisions.

Besides, I no longer work for PiggyBank. I don't have anything to sell you. And you experienced first hand the need to not blindly trust the authority of investment professionals. In the realm of prospecting what the future holds, nobody knows.

Deciding how to invest for the future is taking calculated risk, and it's not easy. But there is something that you can do to give yourself a head start. It's a simple habit."

"What is it?"

"Controlling your expenses and spending less is sometimes more effective than trying to earn more.

A lot of the focus in investing is on what we might gain. But it is also important to keep an eye on the costs we might save."

"What costs are you thinking about?"

"Fees are an important aspect of investing. We pay fees for investment services: on financial advice, on buying and selling, and having our money managed. We either pay them upfront or they are subtracted from our returns. But the cumulated impact of fees on our investment performance can be significant.

Remember how investment returns snowball over time? The fees that we pay are returns that we won't be able to reinvest and won't snowball for us. So we need to make every effort to minimise the fees that we pay whenever possible."

"What fees should I keep in mind?" Socrates asked.

"The first kind is transaction costs.

When you buy and sell stocks, bonds, currencies, properties, collectibles and so on, you may have to pay transaction fees to brokers, banks and agents. Every time you transact in and out of investments, costs add up. So weigh your investment decisions beforehand in order to avoid dealing more frequently than necessary.

The second kind is fund fees.

If you decide to invest in funds, fund managers will charge fees for managing money. The fee structure of a fund is generally a mix of recurring management fees, which the fund charges on the money that you give them to manage regardless of how good the eventual performance is, and sometimes a performance fee. The performance fee is like a bonus paid to the fund manager to reward good management. It is proportional to how much the fund

MINIMISING FEES
CHECKLIST

WATCH OUT FOR:

- [x] TRANSACTION COSTS
- [x] FUND FEES
- [x] TAXES

(THE LESS YOU PAY IN FEES, THE MORE MONEY YOU CAN REINVEST FOR YOURSELF) returns in excess of a pre-agreed threshold. The information that you should look for in the documentation of a fund is the 'total expense ratio'. It is the percentage of your invested money that the fund charges on a recurring basis for overseeing the management of your money.

Lastly, minding your fees means minding the taxes that you pay.

Optimising your taxes is an underrated way of saving precious money which can instead be made to work for you. Pay attention to how income and capital gains on various types of investments are taxed.

The less you pay in fees and taxes, the more money you can reinvest for yourself."

"May I ask you one more question?"

Catsby eased into his chair. "Sure, shoot."

"In our early meetings, there seemed to be this underlying assumption that there was inflation in the economy.

But hearing the recent news, it seems that deflation, not inflation, might become the new normal. There is a chance that we could go through a long period of falling prices, and maybe slow growth if I understand correctly. How would this impact the investment framework?"

"I am glad that you asked the question. You know that improving technology allows companies to produce more with less. In some cases, it can erode salaries and the profit margins of certain companies. So between improving technology and slower demographic growth, we can't exclude that Catland could go through phases where prices are on a sustainable downward path.

The first thing to know is that this does not invalidate what we said earlier about investments. Stocks, bonds, property, foreign exchange, commodities and collectibles still work the same.

What changes in times of deflation is that cash itself becomes more valuable as time goes by. So holding onto cash can be a good investment in times of deflation, as its purchasing power grows over time.

The second thing is that the challenges of managing money remain the same. Investing in other asset classes than cash may still make sense as long as these assets do better than negative inflation. As long as investments offer returns which are above the rate of negative inflation, they would grow your wealth compared to the purchasing power that your savings have today."

Catsby looked at the sky in an ominous way. "But there is one thing that we need to keep high on our minds in times of deflation. It is the reaction of financial authorities and the central bank.

What can potentially accompany negative inflation is negative interest rates. Negative rates are just a form of extra low interest rates to stimulate demand and try and kickstart economic growth. Negative rates mean that lenders pay interest to borrowers to lend them money, and borrowers get paid interest to borrow."

Socrates scratched his head.

"Strange, eh?" Catsby said. "It is possible that at some point, depositors will be asked to pay interest on their savings to leave them at the bank. The problem with this is that it is hard for depositors to accept.

If this were to happen, we could see depositors withdraw their money from banks to avoid paying interest on their deposits and to preserve the value of their money.

Savers and investors could look for alternative ways of storing their wealth in real, tangible assets outside of the traditional financial system.

But such bank runs would risk causing financial instability as they could prompt some banks to fail. So authorities like the government and the central bank might try and do everything they can to prevent this from happening. And believe me, they can be inventive.

They could make the current currency illegal in one form or another. They could introduce a new currency with an expiry date, so we would be forced to spend it soon after receiving it. They could make paper money unavailable so that all payments would have to be electronic, which would be a perfect way of locking the financial system and preventing depositors from withdrawing cash. Or they could simply limit cash withdrawals, so that depositors would have no other choice than accepting the negative rates imposed on the banking system."

"What to do if that were to happen?" Socrates asked.

"Be prepared and be a step ahead," Catsby replied.

"Structural deflation is unchartered territory. But this is why we spoke about contingency plans. We said that there was a case for having investments outside of the traditional financial system for times when the system breaks down. A prudent investor diversifies and will also think about having some alternative stores of value in his portfolio."

Socrates tried to stay composed. Then he asked: "Would you have examples of asset allocations?"

Catsby called the waiter and asked if he could use the black chalkboard, on which they hadn't yet written the menu of the day. The waiter obliged and brought a couple of chalk sticks.

Catsby drew three pie charts on the blackboard. He said: "Here are three examples of portfolio allocations."

The first pie read "stocks". Catsby said, "A portfolio fully allocated to stocks is very aggressive. It is strongly geared towards an improving economy. It will also be volatile, because of the lack of diversification. But some investors swear by it, especially if their goal is the long-term growth of their capital."

The second chart was split in the middle, with 50% stocks and 50% bonds. "The second allocation is an example of a balanced portfolio. Similar weights allocated to both stocks and bonds should provide

PORTFOLIO ALLOCATIONS: EXAMPLES

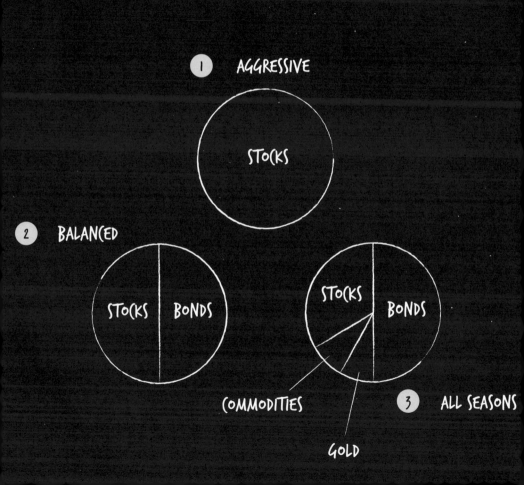

a balance of growth and income, and also some protection of the original capital invested. This portfolio won't be immune to down-moves, but the fluctuations of such a portfolio should be smoother than for a stock-only allocation, as greater diversification stabilises returns."

"How about the third one?" Socrates asked.

"The third pie had four sections: 50% bonds, 30% stocks, 10% gold and 10% commodities." Catsby said: "This could be an example of an 'all seasons' portfolio. The idea is that different asset classes respond to different kinds of economic weather. So such a portfolio might be suited to cope with a broader range of scenarios."

"Should I stick to one of these charts?" Socrates asked.

"These are examples and there is no one-size-fits-all answer. The weights should be adjusted according to investment goals, personal circumstances, and the seasons one expects. If anything, these charts are good conversation starters to engage with a professional adviser or ask yourself relevant questions.

Investing is more art than science. But the fundamental principles remain, and diversifying across different asset classes reduces the chance of concentrating on the wrong allocation.

In the end, asset allocation can be as complicated or as simple as you wish. But if you keep it simple, you will also likely save on fees.

Once you have decided on an allocation which you think is appropriate for you, do not invest all your savings at once. Scale in, and over time, gradually, bit by bit, you will get your wealth allocated in the desired proportions."

"Once my savings are allocated, is there anything I should do?" Socrates asked.

"If you remain happy with your allocation, rebalance your portfolio once in a while. Rebalancing means periodically selling or buying some assets to make sure that the weights of your allocations remain around the desired proportions as time goes.

Mechanically, winning allocations will become a larger portion of your portfolio over time while allocations that perform less well will become a smaller percentage if you do nothing about it."

Socrates nodded.

EPILOGUE:

YOU GOTTA DO WHAT YOU GOTTA DO

Catsby waved at the waiter and asked for the bill.

"Let me have it," Socrates said.

Catsby nodded his thanks.

"What will you do after this?" Socrates asked.

"I don't know. Maybe I will learn design from you?"

Socrates laughed. "May I ask you one more thing?"

"Always."

"I took a lot of your time and you never asked for anything in return.

What was in it for you?"

Catsby smiled.

"It's not all about interest, my friend," he said.

"What then?"

"Good deeds snowball too."

ACKNOWLEDGEMENTS

Here's a big thank you for your vote of confidence, generosity,
leap of faith, words of encouragement, feedback and inspiration.
The Cat & the Banker wouldn't be here without you:

Attila Achenbach, Devika Agarwal, Kenneth Akintewe, Zahia Allain, Bernise
Ang, Chow Yang Ang, Karina Anggono, Karin Aue, Sebastien Auvray, Graham
Bibby, Isobel Black, Cecile Boiron, Ivonne Bojoh, Magali Bonnier, Thomas
Boquien, Arnaud Bourrut Lacouture, Troy Bowler, Rachel Bravard Burke,
Laurent Brighel, Celine Bulard, Ye Cao, Aimee Carmichael, Sharon Casey,
Claire Castera, Nick Cheong, Kit Eng Cho, Thu Ha Chow, Andrea Coiro, Lee
Constantine, Jean-Philippe Crochet, Virgina Cuevas, François de Moulliac,
Sebastien de Peretti, Sophie de Thore, Thomas Decant, Olivier Desbarres,
Philipp Diekhöner, Brett Diment, Xiao Ding, Bill Diviney, Guillaume Faure,
Chengyan Feng, Thomas Flichy, Giorgio Fossi, Oliver Garcia Machin, Fabien
Gerbron, Yenal Ghori, Colin Godbarge, Hui Hoon Goh, Joanne Goh, Jethro
Goodchild, Krishna Goradia, Thomas Gorissen, Matt Grandvallet, Neary
Guenin, Patrice Guesnet, Sarah Guilloto, Murat Gunc, Edwin Gutierrez,
Damien Hamon, Marcel Heijnen, Tareck Horchani, Robert Hostetter, Yebi
Hu, Thierry Huret, Anne Ioos, Manami Ishii, Moyeen Islam, Matei Iurascu,
Bassam Jabry, Emmanuel Jacomy, Lucienne Jallabert, Tom Jennings, Søren
Skov Jensen, Marie-Catherine Jensen, Zhengping Jiang, Mélanie Job, Shalom
Joseph, Grace Juhn, Vaibhav Kamble, Sean Kelly, Thomas Kemmsies, Fleur
Khalil, Karen Khoo, Rak Kim, Wil Kolen, Angela Kuek, Matthieu Lauras,
Mathieu Lebrun, Mei Lin Lee, Sandra Faustina Lee, Sharon Lee, Clemence
Le Floch, Christophe Legaret, Yves & Andrée Legaret, Jeanine & Etienne

Le Garrec, Fabrice Le Geldon, Françoise Le Jannou, Bertrand Le Nezet, Cassandra Leong, Jeff Leung, Roger & Danielle Le Quere, Angele Le Quere-Mehadji, Laurent Levy, Raphael Levy, Guillaume Levy-Lambert, Kyoka Li, Oka Li, Benjamin Liang, Samuel Lim, Han Lin, Kristl Lin, Aaron Xiyue Liu, Aijing Liu, Jin Liu, Widelia Liu, James Lockard, Nicholas Loke, Khashayar Lotfizadeh, Edmund Low, Xinliang Lu, Lin Luo, Harold Ma, Mariko Magnan, Gyanesh Maheshwar, Rupa Majumdar, Jim Malone, Mikael Marguerie, Caroline Mars, Bernard Martelly, Erwin Mayer, Christophe Mayol, Adam McCabe, Kada Mehadji, Nora Mehadji, Emma Meheust, Sherry Mei, Vinod Menon, Olivier Mermet, James Mernagh, Florian Mezy, Romain Michalon, Daryl Mok, Dawn Mok, Christophe Monier, Kailas Moorthy, Djedid Mouhoussoune, Eleonore Mouy, Karim Mrani Alaoui, Andrew Narracott, Melvin Neo, Alexander Ng, Hui Hsien Ng, Joyce Ng, WaiChung Ng, Alfredo Noriega, Jasmeet Notay, Lara Odusanya, Jae-Eun Oh, Mae Ong Gmira, Radhika Pandya, Sejin Park, Martin Pasquier, Hamish Pepper, Claude Pfersdorff, Benoît Pinatelle, Thomas Poinsu, Trevor Pugh, Swati Raghupathy, Max Ruzenberg, Francisco Sacristan, Yoann Sapanel, Neil Schofield, Liana Seah, Omar Selim, Guillaume Servajean, Adeline Setiawan, Muj Sheikh, Tina Shen, Daren Shiau, KJ Sinha, Prakriti Sofat, Jie Song, Paul Stuart, Suhaila Suboh, Sophia Susanto, Kevin Talbot, Guat Kheng Tan, Simon Tan, Gael Tang, David Teeters, Jeremy Teng, Jelly Teo, Bernard Terrill, Charles Tessier, Marilyn Tjitra, Soon Ju Tok, Tamara Trinh, Erica Truong, Esther Tsang, Sze Tsoi, Robin Ucelli, Marnie Uy, Patrick van Dam, Hans van der Putten, Edo van Dijk, Geert van Kuijk, Per van Spall, Julien Vergues, Mathieu Verlaet, Guillaume Viel, Thorsten Vieth, Guy Vincent, Varong Vongsinudom, Mark Vreeswijk, Amandine Wang, Lai Wei, Tom White, Erly Witoyo, Dan Wong, Simon Wong, Glen Woodmansee, Shyue Woon, Danqing Wu, Echo Qie Yang, Jahan Yang Mehadji, Kaitlyn Yang, Ruishi Yang, Murni Yanti, Li Li Yeo, Joanne Yip, Debby Yu, Si Qi Yuen, Smaïn Zemmerli, Mu Yang Zhang, Tong Zhao and Juemin Zhu.